⊄⊞B The Practitioner's Bookshelf

Hands-On Language and Literacy Books for Classroom Teachers and Administrators

Dorothy S. Strickland
FOUNDING EDITOR, LANGUAGE AND LITERACY SERIES

Celia Genishi and Donna E. Alvermann
LANGUAGE AND LITERACY SERIES EDITORS*

RTI and the Adolescent Reader:
Responsive Literacy Instruction in Secondary Schools
William G. Brozo

Let's Poem:
The Essential Guide to Teaching Poetry in a High-Stakes, Multimodal World
Mark Dressman

Literacy in the Welcoming Classroom:
Creating Family–School Partnerships That Support Student Learning
JoBeth Allen

DIY Media in the Classroom: New Literacies Across Content Areas
Barbara Guzzetti, Kate Elliott, and Diana Welsch

Bring It to Class: Unpacking Pop Culture in Literacy Learning
Margaret C. Hagood, Donna E. Alvermann, and Alison Heron-Hruby

The Reading Turn-Around: A Five-Part Framework for Differentiated Instruction
Stephanie Jones, Lane W. Clarke, and Grace Enriquez

Academic Literacy for English Learners:
High-Quality Instruction Across Content Areas
Cynthia Brock, Diane Lapp, Rachel Salas, and Dianna Townsend

Literacy for Real: Reading, Thinking, and Learning in the Content Areas
ReLeah Cossett Lent

Teaching Individual Words: One Size Does Not Fit All
Michael F. Graves

Literacy Essentials for English Language Learners: Successful Transitions
Maria Uribe and Sally Nathenson-Mejía

Literacy Leadership in Early Childhood: The Essential Guide
Dorothy S. Strickland and Shannon Riley-Ayers

---

* For a list of current titles in the Language and Literacy Series, see *www.tcpress.com*

RTI and the Adolescent Reader

Responsive Literacy Instruction in Secondary Schools

WILLIAM G. BROZO

Foreword by Richard L. Allington

Teachers College
Columbia University
New York and London

INTERNATIONAL
Reading Association
800 BARKSDALE ROAD, PO BOX 8139
NEWARK, DE 19714-8139, USA (302) 731-1600
www.reading.org

Published simultaneously by Teachers College Press, 1234 Amsterdam Avenue, New York, NY 10027, and the International Reading Association, 800 Barksdale Road, P.O. Box 8139, Newark, DE 19714-8139

Library of Congress Cataloging-in-Publication Data

Brozo, William G.
    RTI and the adolescent reader : responsive literacy instruction in secondary schools / William G. Brozo; foreword by Richard L. Allington.
        p. cm. — (The practitioner's bookshelf)
Includes bibliographical references and index.
ISBN 978-0-8077-5230-2 (pbk. : alk. paper)
    1. Remedial teaching—United States. 2. Education, Secondary—United States. 3. School failure—United States—Prevention. 4. School improvement programs—United States. 5. Response to intervention (Learning disabled children). I. Title.
    LB1029.R4B779   2011
    373.190973—dc22   2011005011

ISBN 978-0-8077-5230-2 (paper)

Printed on acid-free paper
Manufactured in the United States of America

18   17   16   15   14   13   12   11   8   7   6   5   4   3   2   1

Contents

Foreword *by Richard L. Allington* vii

Introduction 1

1. **What Is RTI in Literacy?** 7

  RTI: A Model in Search of Validation 8

  A Brief History of RTI 8

  Components of RTI 12

  Chapter Summary 21

2. **Problems Applying RTI in
Literacy at the Secondary Level** 23

  Struggling Adolescent Readers and RTI 24

  The Complexity of American Secondary Schools 26

  Structural Conditions 28

  School Culture and Teacher Identity 37

  Support Structures 39

  The Complexity of Adolescence 45

  Chapter Summary 48

3. **Reframing RTI as Responsive Literacy
Instruction for All Adolescent Readers** 50

  Response to Intervention or Responsive Instruction? 50

  Envisionments of Responsive Literacy Instruction 53

  Achieving a Comprehensive and Responsive
Literacy Program at the Secondary Level 61

Expanding Students' Literacy Capacities
at All Levels with Responsive Instruction   73

Creative Services for Meeting the Needs
of Students with Serious Reading Difficulties   86

Chapter Summary   103

**4. RTI for Secondary Literacy:
Analysis of School Cases**   **106**

Analysis of School Cases of RTI for Secondary Literacy   108

Case #1 Liberty Middle School, Hanover County, Virginia   108

Case #2 Lincoln Public Schools, Lincoln, Nebraska   115

Case #3 San Diego Unified School District,
San Diego, California   123

Chapter Summary   129

**5. RTI for Secondary Literacy:
Where Do We Go from Here?**   **131**

Looking Back to See Forward   132

Is RTI for Secondary Literacy Worth Salvaging?   134

Chapter Summary   142

References   **145**

Index   **159**

About the Author   **168**

Foreword

BILL BROZO HAS WRITTEN an honest and useful text for teachers working with adolescent students. His focus is on the new Response to Intervention (RTI) initiative, recently created by Congress in an attempt to improve reading achievement and reduce the numbers of students classified as having disabilities. Of special interest are students classified, or who may be classified, as learning disabled (LD). Today roughly half of all pupils with disabilities are students classified as learning disabled. In fact, growth in the numbers of pupils identified as LD has been quite spectacular, considering that there were *no* LD students prior to 1975, when Congress created that label!

The primary characteristic of students identified as LD is their low level of reading proficiency. Unfortunately, identifying poor readers as LD has not served them well. The reading instruction they have been provided has been described by researchers as being of both lower quality and shorter duration than the reading lessons provided typical students in their general education classrooms (Allington & McGill-Franzen, 1989a, 1989b; Vaughn & Linan-Thompson, 2003; Vaughn, Moody, & Schumm, 1998; Ysseldyke, Thurlow, Mecklenburg & Graden, 1984).

Brozo notes that the most important tier in the RTI process is Tier 1, the classroom instruction that students participate in. An alternative way of suggesting this is to note that struggling readers need high-quality lessons all day long. I have also made this point (Allington, 2008). However, as Brozo notes, few adolescents attend schools where much attention is given to the quality of instruction that struggling readers receive. Instead, those who teach adolescents pay more attention to grade-level content standards. Brozo notes that middle and high schools are more committed to content learning than most elementary schools are, where the focus is on student development. Perhaps because of this focus, high schools are more complicated places to teach than elementary schools.

Brozo makes two central arguments in this book. First, middle and high schools cannot simply attempt to replicate RTI models shown to be effective in elementary schools. Second, these schools must begin to do something that produces greater learning in low-achieving students, including students with disabilities.

At the same time, he argues that almost everything we know about teaching struggling readers and designing RTI models is derived from studies of students below grade 6. That is, there are virtually no studies of either reading intervention programs for adolescents or RTI efforts with older students. He notes that adolescent reading interventions that emphasize decoding development have not produced students who read with comprehension. Of course, reading with comprehension is the single goal of adolescent literacy development.

What Brozo proposes is a schoolwide focus on adolescent literacy development, including professional development for content teachers that provides the needed knowledge and skills to develop lessons that benefit all students, including students who struggle with reading. He presents case studies of three diverse high schools, each using a different strategy in an RTI framework. He notes that these schools had varied success in meeting the needs of struggling readers, and offers advice on how each model might be improved.

As you read this book consider the current situation of struggling readers in your school. Consider also the ideas and strategies that Brozo offers to guide your planning of any new initiative designed to address the needs of your struggling readers. Students deserve the best education we can provide, even struggling readers. Brozo provides a powerful framework for moving in that direction.

—Richard L. Allington, PhD, University of Tennessee

Introduction

IT IS DIFFICULT TO DENY that many U.S. middle and high school students are in need of special literacy supports.

- Approximately two-thirds of 8th- and 12th-grade students read at less than the "proficient" level on the National Assessment of Educational Progress (Rampey, Dion, & Donahue, 2009).
- 15-year-olds rank slightly below average in reading literacy on PISA (Program for International Student Assessment) as compared with 65 other nations, marking no improvement in a decade relative to our global peers.
- Nearly 32% of high school graduates are not adequately prepared for college-level English composition courses (ACT, 2005).

- Approximately 40% of high school graduates lack the literacy skills employers seek (National Education Summit on High Schools, 2005).
- About 1.2 million students drop out annually, and their literacy skills are lower than most industrialized nations (Laird, DeBell, Kienzl, & Chapman, 2007; Organisation for Economic Co-Operation and Development [OECD], 2001).

In no small way, these and other indicators of declining literacy achievement have shifted national attention toward struggling and striving adolescent readers. Proposed federal initiatives such as the PASS Act (which foundered in the Senate) and now the LEARN Act, would fund literacy programs in middle and high schools. No Child Left Behind (NCLB), originally passed to boost reading achievement for children in the elementary grades, was expanded in NCLB's reauthorization to include support for older *striving* readers.

Whether these attempts at addressing the needs of struggling adolescent readers will bear fruit is still uncertain. One thing is certain, however: Concern for the literacy development of students beyond the elementary years is not likely to fade any time soon as our nation continues to compete in an ever-more fierce global economy. As a result, U.S. secondary schools have been under growing pressure to find ways of improving the reading and writing performance of youth.

One federal initiative that has been the most influential on the nature and structure of programs for secondary literacy is the Individuals with Disabilities Education Act (IDEA) (U.S. Department of Education, 2004). Its reauthorization in 2004 contains regulations for a Response to Intervention (RTI) approach as an alternative to the IQ discrepancy method for identifying students who may be eligible for specific learning disability services, including reading. Almost overnight, across the country, first elementary schools and now secondary schools that previously had no structured literacy programs began adopting the RTI model.

Response to Intervention is described as a multi-tiered, preventive approach to supporting students' learning needs (Cortiella, 2005; Fuchs, Mock, Morgan, & Young, 2003). Coinciding with the rise of Reading First–endorsed approaches to primary-level literacy interventions, RTI has become an increasingly common framework for addressing students' reading problems in elementary school (Batsche et al., 2005). Teachers and administrators across the United States have devoted considerable time and energy to designing and implementing reading intervention programs based on the tiered approach of RTI (Allington & Walmsley, 2007; Fuchs & Fuchs, 2005).

According to the "what's hot" poll (Cassidy & Cassidy, 2009), RTI is one of the hottest topics in the literacy field. But even as RTI spreads like wildfire, voices of caution are starting to be raised. Reynolds and Shaywitz (2009) point out that:

> Although the notion of RTI as a process of service delivery may have potential to be helpful to both regular education and special education, the extant evidence does not support the seemingly unbridled enthusiasm for its current readiness status from its proponents who appear to have been overly optimistic and often incomplete in their presentations of the RTI model, with regard to its research support, ease of implementation, breadth of applications in them of what constitutes responsiveness. (p. 134)

Because RTI-inspired programs have become so widespread (Fuchs & Deshler, 2007), and due to the fact that RTI overlaps with issues of language and literacy (Strangeman, Hitchcock, Hall, Meo, & Coyne, 2006), the International Reading Association established an RTI commission that set guiding principles for literacy professionals, learning specialists, general education teachers, administrators, and others (IRA Commission on RTI, 2009). Within the six proposed principles comes the commission's admonishment that:

> Approaches to RTI must be sensitive to developmental differences in language and literacy among students at different ages and grades. Although many prevailing approaches to RTI focus on the early elementary grades, it is essential for teachers and support personnel at middle and secondary levels to provide their students with the language and literacy instruction they need to succeed in school and beyond. (p. 6)

As national attention continues to shift in the direction of struggling and striving adolescent readers, interest in the utility of RTI at the secondary level continues to grow (Duffy, n.d.). The IRA

Commission's recommendation is critical because it warns of the proclivity of some districts and schools to institute RTI at the secondary level based on primary/elementary approaches. Within elementary-level, self-contained classrooms, implementation of RTI-like tiered interventions has proven possible (Fuchs & Fuchs, 2005). Little research is currently available, however, on the use of RTI in secondary schools (Cobb, Sample, Alwell, & Johns, 2005). Thus, in the absence of research and scholarship around RTI for adolescent literacy, it falls to middle and high schools to devise their own approaches to implementing responsive tiered interventions for youth.

PURPOSE AND ORGANIZATION OF
RTI AND THE ADOLESCENT READER

In this book I explore the efficacy of an RTI approach for meeting the literacy needs of secondary students. I begin by briefly tracing the history of RTI and providing a clear explanation of the approach. Next, I examine how RTI has come to be considered a viable intervention model for adolescent readers. I go on to analyze the feasibility of RTI at the secondary level by considering authentic structural, political, cultural, as well as teacher and student identity issues unique to secondary schools that pose challenges to tiered and comprehensive intervention for literacy. Finally, I examine realistic approaches to making RTI an effective framework for responsive literacy instruction at the secondary level. Actual secondary school cases demonstrating tiered interventions are described and analyzed.

The content of the book is evidence-based, drawing on the research literature on RTI and adolescent literacy assessment and instruction. It also relies on informed, expert opinion, as well as the practical knowledge of school insiders. My goal has been to maintain a familiar tone to reach a broad audience of practitioners, school leaders, and policymakers.

Each chapter contains helpful organizational and learning features. Chapters are introduced with a Highlights box that foreshadows the critical content, and conclude with a Summary. Also at the end of each chapter is the Relate to Integrate feature, which poses questions and prompts that foster critical thinking and application of chapter ideas. Another important feature within Chapters 1–4 is RTI in the Real World. In these boxes you will find descriptions of actual secondary schools employing an RTI for literacy approach. These descriptions are followed by Critical Questions about aspects of RTI at the school.

This book is neither a paean to nor a polemic of Response to Intervention (RTI). Instead, it offers a legitimate critique of RTI for secondary literacy, as well as a possible vision of RTI in which the central aim is to ensure all adolescents are provided quality instructional practices and have rewarding learning experiences that are responsive to their unique needs and promote genuine literacy growth.

CHAPTER 1

What Is RTI in Literacy?

HIGHLIGHTS

- Response to Intervention (RTI) as proposed in special education legislation is meant to prevent and address the literacy and learning difficulties of students.
- RTI as a system of progress monitoring and responsive interventions for secondary literacy is still in need of validation.
- There are few practical models of RTI for secondary literacy.
- RTI at the secondary level may be possible if reframed as a comprehensive program that provides responsive literacy instruction to students at all ability levels, whether they are learning disabled or not.

RTI: A MODEL IN SEARCH OF VALIDATION

IN SPITE OF THE ENTHUSIASM for Response to Intervention (RTI), it is necessary to point out that even its staunchest advocates (c.f., Barnett, Daly, Jones, & Lentz, 2004; Fuchs, Mock, Morgan, & Young, 2003; Gresham, 2001; Vaughn & Fuchs, 2003) agree that RTI is far from a clearly structured, highly research-validated program with universally agreed-upon features; RTI is still more rhetoric than reality, still more of a work in progress than a refined and developed product. This is especially true where secondary literacy is concerned (Brozo, 2009/2010). It is unfortunate, then, that many books and articles about RTI describe it as though it is a well-established system. This is important to bear in mind as you read the following brief history of RTI and the description of the elements, such as universal screening, progress monitoring, and tiered interventions that are often recommended but are not as often observed.

A BRIEF HISTORY OF RTI

Where did RTI come from? To answer this question, it's helpful to include a historical context. In 1976, with the passage of the landmark Public Law 94-142, the Federal government began supporting special education services in the United States. This legislation was renewed in 1990 with the Individuals with Disabilities Act, more popularly known by its acronym, IDEA. In 1997, when IDEA was reauthorized, 13 categories of disability were identified in the Act. The largest and most confounding category in terms of identification is Learning Disabilities (LD), which accounts for over 50% of all students served under the Act (Gresham, 2001).

The definition of learning disability has changed very little since the label was originally used in 1963 (Ysseldyke & Marston, 1999) and appears now in IDEA:

> a disorder in one or more of the basic psychological processes involved in understanding or in using language, spoken or written, which may manifest itself in an imperfect ability to listen, think, speak, read, write, spell or to do mathematical calculations. [P.L. 94-142, 121a. 5b(9)]

As to the eligibility issue, IDEA 1997 stipulated a problem-solving approach be used, but the original PL 94-142 operational definition remained (Bradley, Danielson, & Doolittle, 2007):

> (2) The team finds that a child has a severe discrepancy between achievement and intellectual ability in one or more of the following areas: (i) Oral expression. (ii) Listening comprehension. (iii) Written expression. (iv) Basic reading skill. (v) Reading comprehension. (p. 9)

Gresham (2001) suggests that because of inconsistent application of this definition, a very large proportion of the school-identified LD population would fail to meet federal eligibility criteria. At the heart of the problem with identification is an over-reliance on intelligence and achievement tests, both of which can have considerable measurement error. Also, as a technical matter, students who exhibit low scores on both intelligence and achievement may be ineligible for services if the ability-to-achievement gap is not large enough, even though the student's low scores would argue for needed learning support. At the same time, students with high intelligence scores but unmotivated and low-achieving outcomes or those with limited knowledge of English have been prone to misidentification (Harry & Klingner, 2007).

The reauthorization of IDEA 1997 in 2004 brought with it specific language that called for classifying learning disabled students based on documentation of how well they respond to interventions—this is the process we now commonly refer to as RTI (Fuchs & Fuchs, 2006; Gersten & Dimino, 2006; Mastropieri & Scruggs, 2005). RTI doesn't replace the intelligence-achievement discrepancy approach, but provides an alternative to learning disabilities identification for schools and systems. In its pristine form, RTI entails initial universal screening (essentially, testing of all students) to determine which students may be exhibiting a learning problem, followed by different tiers of intervention depending upon the severity of need, accompanied by frequent assessments to track progress and/or modify interventions. This last feature is critical because there was a focused effort in IDEA 2004 to shift attention away from monitoring paperwork and compliance regulations to monitoring student progress in academic areas (Gersten, Compton, Connor, Dimino, Santoro, Linan-Tompson, & Tilly, 2008).

There are varying opinions about the inception of RTI. According to Wright (2007), it dates back at least to the middle of the 20th century, with the rise in influence of applied behavior analysis (Baer, Wolf, & Risley, 1968). Behavior analysis in education has found its full expression in the area of special education with such approaches as direct instruction and precision teaching. By the 1980s, academic monitoring tools were being developed to determine the effectiveness of behavioral-type interventions (Deno, 1986; Shinn, 1989). In 1991, Gresham introduced the phrase *resistance to intervention* to describe students who failed to demonstrate expected positive academic behavior based on interventions and progress monitoring, the essence of RTI was formed, and soon after, *resistance* evolved into *response.*

Others suggest that RTI's roots go much further back than applied behaviorism. Because RTI is also called the problem-solving approach, it has been compared with the scientific method used to study natural phenomena (Wedl, 2005), particularly because the wording in IDEA 2004 stipulates the use of scientific, research-based interventions. According to this approach, a problem or phenomenon is identified, a hypothesis is formed, study procedures are implemented, data are collected and analyzed, and finally interpretations and conclusions are derived. Thus, when a similar systematic approach is applied to student learning (Tilly, Reschly, & Grimes, 1999), teachers might begin by asking: 1. What is the problem? This could be followed by 2. Why does the problem exist? then 3. What should be done to address the problem? and finally 4. Did the intervention work and if not, what other interventions should be tried?

In educational settings, an answer to the first question, *What is the problem?* is obtained through teacher observations, performance records, test scores, etc. For example, Dominic's 7th-grade reading/language arts teacher notices soon into the new school year that he is struggling with the poems, passages, and plays in their literature book. Dominic's answers to questions about the readings reflect limited recall and understanding. She looks up his reading test scores, which indicate that his achievement level is 2 years below his grade placement. These data corroborate her observations that Dominic is in need of extra reading support.

As to the second question, *Why does the problem exist?*, the language arts teacher notes that Dominic, for whom this is his 1st year at her school, has attended at least four other schools in the district, three of which were classified as low-performing. This leads to the conjecture that Dominic has not received regular skills monitoring and consistent quality instruction.

The third important question, *What should be done to address the problem?* gets at the intervention plan for students experiencing barriers to effective reading and learning. Dominic's language arts teacher exercises a range of options. First, she talks with the school's reading coach, who urges her to try to implement strategies and practices within the classroom to improve Dominic's performance. They reflect on specific areas of need he is exhibiting. According to the language arts teacher, he appears to have adequate decoding skills but doesn't know the meaning of many grade-appropriate words and finds it difficult to remember important details or infer main ideas. Together, the language arts teacher and reading coach craft a plan for Dominic that focuses on vocabulary development and comprehension skills. The teacher uses a combination of whole- and small-group instruction as well as individual assistance to support Dominic.

Once a specific instructional plan is initiated, it is necessary to consider the final question in this approach: *Did the intervention work and if not, what other interventions should be tried?* To determine the effectiveness of an ongoing intervention student performance on tasks related to the development of targeted skills needs to be monitored regularly. In Dominic's case, the language arts teacher decided to monitor progress with existing curriculum-based measures, such as daily home- and in-class work, quizzes, and tests. The hope and expectation is that Dominic will benefit indirectly and directly from the increase in instructional time on ways of acquiring word knowledge and making meaning from text, and that this will be evidenced on assignment and test scores.

This approach to responding in a systematic fashion to Dominic's reading needs is the essence of RTI. To be sure, teachers like Dominic's language arts teacher have always used methods and strategies targeted to support individual student's development of needed skills and abilities in reading, math, and other areas of learning. Likewise, teachers and schools have used curriculum-based assessments and other measures to report on student progress. RTI is different in that its advocates talk about it as an institutionalized, systematic, data-driven approach to determine which students may need extra support and to ensure appropriate levels of support are made available to those students (Fletcher, Coulter, Reschly, & Vaughn, 2004). It is meant as a comprehensive early detection and prevention approach that identifies struggling students, like Dominic, and assists them before they fall further behind. Furthermore, the interventions, according to RTI purists, cannot be any strategies or practices, but ones that must have a scientific basis, meaning they must have a record of effectiveness for the students of concern as documented in randomized controlled trial studies.

COMPONENTS OF RTI

Although the specific features of RTI systems vary across states, districts, and schools, there are common components and processes shared by all who employ the approach. These include some form of universal screening, progress monitoring, and tiered interventions.

Universal Screening and Progress Monitoring

Advocates of RTI assert that the traditional approach to identifying students with learning difficulties is flawed because too much time is wasted "waiting for students to fail." In contrast, a system that includes frequent testing and monitoring is presumed to improve the chances of early detection of students in need of extra learning supports (Marshall, 2006; Mellard & Johnson, 2008). Thus, initial universal screening and progress monitoring are the core features of any RTI program. Without this information, it is argued, teachers would not know the type and intensity of intervention struggling students would need. Universal screening means all students are assessed at the beginning of a new school year, and preferably again in the winter and spring (Applebaum, 2009), to determine who may be the target for interventions. Because any kind of testing, especially testing of all students, is potentially costly and time-consuming (Brozo & Hargis, 2003), many school systems rely on convenience data, such as extant standardized test scores from state- or district-level high-stakes assessments to make initial decisions about the type and intensity of academic interventions.

To make screening and progress monitoring more efficient and less of a drain on school resources, Curriculum-Based Measures

(CBMs) have been recommended in place of formal, commercial assessment products (Shinn, 2007). Because curriculum-based measures are created from the very materials teachers and students read and work with daily (Jones, 2009), they are thought to be ecologically valid forms of assessment that offer the possibility of providing teachers insights into student performance that can directly inform instruction.

Two of the more common CBMs are maze tasks and Oral Reading Fluency (ORF) checks. Maze requires students to read a passage in which every *n*th word or a particular type of word has been deleted. When students come to the blank space, they must select answers to multiple-choice items, one of which is the correct word. Maze passages can be extracted directly from the texts students are reading in the classroom, thus making them easy to devise. Another advantage of the maze approach to curriculum-based assessment is that it's possible to administer maze passages to an entire class or group at one time. For example, maze-formatted passages can be distributed like any other paper-and-pencil test or projected from a SMARTboard or onto a screen for any number of desired students to complete. Another advantage of maze problems is that they are a putative assessment of reading comprehension, since students need to understand word, sentence, and overall passage meaning in order to complete each maze task (Brozo & Afflerbach, 2011). Maze tasks have been well-documented in the research literature as a viable approach to reading assessment (DuBay, 2004; Madelaine & Wheldall, 2004).

Oral reading fluency (ORF) checks streamline the screening and monitoring process even more. As with maze tasks, virtually any text can serve as the source material for an ORF assessment, since the process typically involves a student giving a 1-minute timed oral reading. How accurately, rapidly, and expressively—that is, how fluently—a student reads a text will depend on the student's word recognition, print knowledge, and print experience skills (Hasbrouck & Tindal, 2006). It has been asserted that the more automatic these fundamental reading skills are, the more cognitive energy is reserved for thinking about and comprehending text (Tractenberg, 2002). The opposite may be true, as well. If a student has limited automaticity with fluency-related skills, then less cognitive capacity is available for the most important work of reading—comprehension (Strong, Wehby, Falk, & Lane, 2004). It is presumed that because a

(text continues on p. 16)

RTI in the Real World

SPRINGFIELD AND CHICOPEE SCHOOL DISTRICTS, MASSACHUSETTS

The Springfield and Chicopee school districts in Massachusetts are partners in a 5-year grant funded by the Department of Education from 2006–2011. These two districts have a total of six high schools, five of which are participating in the reading intervention study (three schools in Springfield and two in Chicopee). Springfield Public Schools met no NCLB aggregate or subgroup levels for 2006–2008 and Chicopee Public Schools met NCLB aggregate standards in 2007–2008, but no subgroup standards in 2006–2008.

Incoming 9th-grade populations are channeled into three intervention groups: Tier 1 (whole-school) intervention, and Tier 2 (targeted intervention) that used two different intervention programs in each school—specifically Read 180® and Xtreme Reading. Students are considered eligible for targeted intervention participation based on results from the Stanford Diagnostic Reading Test, 4th edition (SDRT-4) which is also used to measure outcome scores at the end of each year.

Whole-School Evaluation Design Overview: Teachers underwent two initial and two ongoing training sessions during the 1st year of implementing the Strategic Model Content Enhancement Routines for Teachers (SIM-CERT) program. They were required to attend two additional training sessions in Year 2. A majority of teachers met minimum requirements for classroom-level implementation in Year 2 by using the Unit Organizer routine encouraged by their professional development sessions.

SIM-CERT, developed by the University of Kansas' Center for Research on Learning, is designed to be a series of ubiquitous activities that teachers use to examine their instruction and provide content literacy interventions regardless of their instructional content. Three activities are stressed: evaluation of content, determination of what students need to achieve success, and implementation of routines that support students as they apply appropriate techniques.

Read 180: Read 180 uses authentic situations to help students practice noticing and resolving literacy problems. It incorporates computer-assisted technology to track individual student progress and adjust reading instruction accordingly (an animated tutor). Materials targeted for adolescents focus on the fundamentals of reading: phonics, fluency, vocabulary, comprehension, spelling, writing, and grammar. Lessons are designed for 90-minute blocks. Teachers direct whole-group instruction for the first 20 minutes and the last 10 minutes. The time in between is spent rotating among three stations: independent reading, computer-assisted learning, and small-group instruction directed by the teacher.

Xtreme Reading: This program targets students who read above a Grade 4 level, but fall 2 years or more below their own grade-level reading expectations. Xtreme Reading focuses on explicit strategy instruction, relying on metacognition training that teaches students to transfer their literacy awareness across academic learning situations. At the beginning of the year, students are taught how to create a positive learning environment and what is expected of them and their behavior as learners in various situations—lectures, discussions, independent work, and small-group work. This focus on behavior and motivation fills the first 4 weeks of the program. After this initial section, lessons shift to focus on seven reading strategies: LINCS Vocabulary, Word Mapping, Word Identification, Self-Questioning, Visual Imagery, Paraphrasing, and Inference. The first three strategies focus on vocabulary and the last four target reading comprehension. Teachers explicitly model strategies for students and integrate teaching the writing process across the whole year of instruction. The teaching methods used are whole-class discussions, explicit modeling, guided practice activities, paired-student practice, and independent practice.

Assessments: The Xtreme Reading and Read 180 programs both come with their own progress-monitoring assessments. Thus, there is no whole-school reading evaluation test aside from the SRDT-4 given at the end of each year.

CRITICAL QUESTIONS

The Springfield and Chicopee school districts approach to RTI places a great deal of responsibility on the classroom teacher.

- Do you think the required training sessions for teachers were adequate? What would you recommend for improving teacher training?
- What type of supports could be put in place at the Springfield and Chicopee School Districts to ensure teachers had ongoing assistance in implementing the SIM-CERT approach?
- What challenges are likely for Springfield and Chicopee math and chemistry teachers in applying the SIM-CERT approach?

reasonably close relationship has been established between reading fluency and overall reading achievement (Rasinski, Retzel, Chard, & Linan-Thompson, 2011), ORF checks provide valid indicators of the effectiveness of interventions focused on increasing reading ability (Shinn, 1998; Stecker & Fuchs, 2000).

Specifically, ORF is determined by words correct per minute (WCPM), which tells both teacher and student how many words can be read correctly in 1 minute. A student reads aloud while a teacher records any miscues or deviations from the cued text. After 1 minute, the total number of miscues is subtracted from the total number of words read to derive a WCPM score. This score along with all other WCPM checks can be charted on a graph to allow the teacher and the student to see changes and, ideally, growth.

In spite of the relative ease of formatting classroom texts for CBMs—such as maze tasks and ORF checks to monitor struggling readers' progress—expecting all secondary teachers at Tier 1 (that is, all classroom content-area teachers) to construct these assessments and administer them with regularity and fidelity may prove unrealistic. This might help explain in part why there are so few examples of actual RTI programs at the secondary level, particularly in high schools. This issue, along with other curricular and instructional issues related to the uniqueness of secondary school cultures, will be taken up in the next chapter.

Tiered Interventions

If RTI is to be truly responsive, then the initiative must address the learning needs of all students within the most supportive learning contexts schools can offer. The prevalent approach to differentiated interventions is the commonly recommended three-tiered system (Bender & Shores, 2007; Fuchs & Fuchs, 2006; Vaughn, Linan-Thompson, & Hickman, 2003). Using so-called scientifically valid curricula (Brown-Chidsey & Steege, 2005; Daly, Martens, Barnet, Witt, & Olson, 2007; Johnson, Mellard, Fuchs, & McKnight, 2006), teachers and specialists at each tier are to respond to students' learning needs with increasingly intense and targeted supports.

The first tier represents instruction and services available to all students, generally provided at the classroom level. The second tier targets short-term instruction for small groups of students who need extra help. Instruction for select groups of students may occur within and/or outside the classroom. The third tier represents the most intensive level of instruction and is usually provided in a one-to-one context. Students receive different tiers of support depending on how they respond to interventions at any one level. Furthermore, interventions are cumulative as opposed to mutually exclusive, so an especially needy student may be receiving supports at all three tiers simultaneously.

It is important to point out that IDEA 2004 says nothing about a tiered intervention approach to meeting the needs of learning disabled students. In fact, there are no specifications at all in IDEA as to how school systems address students' learning problems or which particular programs or practices are to be used, except that they have their basis in scientific research. Thus, there is nothing "magical" about three levels, and some RTI programs include more or fewer intervention strata (Bender & Shores, 2007). Indeed, even the scientific basis of RTI as a viable approach to decreasing the prevalence of LD is yet unconfirmed (Bender, Ulmer, Baskette, & Shores, 2007). Finally, the question of whether there is, in fact, any actual difference between interventions for non-special education and special education students in Tiers 1 and 2 has not been satisfactorily answered. This is no small matter, as there is a proclivity for reading programs and practices designed originally for special education populations to become part of the general language arts curriculum. The special education-general education drift in reading will be explored in more detail later in this chapter.

Tier I. At this level, intervention resources are supposed to be available to all students within the regular classroom structure (Kovaleski, 2003). If RTI is indeed a preventive approach to reading and learning failure, then realizing an effective RTI program for secondary literacy means middle and high school content-area teachers must possess the skill, will, and ability to meet the reading and learning needs of each of their students (Brozo, 2009/2010; Tomlinson, 2001). This is an enormous responsibility for any teacher, but most especially for the secondary teacher.

In elementary-level, self-contained classrooms, a teacher may have a single group of students the entire day. Providing whole-class, small-group, and individualized reading instruction is not only possible within that setting; it is an expectation. Additionally, weaving the language arts into all aspects of the curriculum is readily achieved in typical early-grades classrooms. In contrast, consider someone like a 10th-grade American history teacher working in a block schedule. He sees a group of students every other day, is under strong pressure to cover the content standards and grade-level expectations of American history, and may only be superficially knowledgeable of and less experienced with linking content literacy strategies to daily instruction. Furthermore, based on my experience, this typical high school teacher is likely to see himself first and foremost as a specialist in history content, which he imparts through whole-group lessons, and provides help over that same content to individual students who seek it. Students who need extra literacy and learning supports are referred to other high school specialists, such as the reading and special education teacher. (The influence of teacher identity and self-efficacy issues, as well as the structure and culture of secondary schools on RTI approaches, will be taken up in more detail in subsequent chapters.)

Tier 2. For students who fail to make expected progress given classroom-level interventions, additional supports are made available (Batsche, 2005). These extra supports most often are provided to small groups or individuals either by the same Tier 1 classroom teacher, specialist, or other academic support staff. Tier 2 interventions are meant to supplement those being received in the classroom, though in some cases, Tier 2 interventions will replace Tier 1 instruction in a format similar to a traditional pull-out approach. The goal is to provide supplemental instruction for only as long as it's necessary for students to begin making normal academic progress.

My comments in connection to Tier 1 for secondary literacy are germane to Tier 2, particularly when the classroom teacher is responsible for Tier 2 learning supports. Reflecting again on our 10th-grade history teacher referred to above, it is enough to ask him to provide evidence-based strategies to all his students, to differentiate instruction for individuals, and to monitor progress with CBMs created from his class texts—all in addition to covering his history content standards. To then ask the history teacher to provide a select number of his students additional reading and learning supports within or beyond the classroom context would seem more than one could reasonably expect.

Tier 3. In this cascading model of RTI, students who fail to respond adequately to interventions within Tier 1 and 2 contexts are given more intensive instruction (Stecker, 2007). This level is usually reserved for one-on-one work with students who have the most severe and chronic reading and learning difficulties. If a student who meets the criteria for Tier 3 services hasn't been evaluated for special education, an Individualized Educational Plan (IEP) meeting is often called (McCook, 2006). The members of this IEP team, it is recommended (Applebaum, 2009), should first determine if any errors were made on progress-monitoring measures or whether interventions were applied with fidelity. Only afterward, if no inconsistencies or problems are noted, should the student be recommended for an evaluation to determine eligibility for special education services. Tier 3 interventions are typically offered by a literacy specialist or LD teacher, and the duration of instruction may last weeks, depending on the student's needs.

For now, let's agree that it is easy to conceptualize a tiered approach to RTI, but daunting from a practical standpoint to transform such an idea into an authentic prevention and intervention system for adolescent reading in middle and high schools. In the next chapter, we'll take a closer look at the complexities of implementing a three-tiered system of reading intervention in a typical secondary school environment, as well as alternative approaches to designing and delivering interventions.

Drifting from Elementary to Secondary and Special Education to General Education

One might speculate that if a system like RTI could find full expression in every primary and elementary school across the country, it could obviate the need for developmental and compensatory reading programs for secondary students. In spite of the fact that far too little research and curricular attention has been given to RTI in middle and high school (Duffy, n.d.), architects and advocates of RTI-like systems are convinced of its viability at this level for early identification of students with reading and learning problems and providing the most efficacious learning environment to boost needed skills.

In the absence of research and documented successes, particularly at the secondary level, it falls to middle and high schools to devise their own approaches to implementing responsive tiered interventions for adolescent literacy (Shanklin, 2008). And this is ironic, because the provision in IDEA stresses the need for RTI programs to be supported by scientific, research-based intervention. Nonetheless, even though there is a lack of scientific evidence for secondary-level RTI, numerous middle and high schools across the United States are moving ahead with tiered approaches to instructional intervention similar to those found in the early grades. The proclivity of some districts and schools to institute RTI at the secondary level based on approaches being used in primary- and elementary-school settings has brought a note of caution from The International Reading Association's RTI Commission (2009). There are several reasons why the Commission's warning is valid based on structural, curricular, and cultural differences between primary/elementary and secondary school contexts. These differences will be considered in-depth in the next chapter.

Of equal concern to the migration upward of RTI-like approaches from primary/elementary grades to middle/high school is the evolution of RTI from special education to general education. Remember, once IDEA 2004 gave the green light, RTI was conceived as the effective alternative to intelligence testing and the discrepancy formula for classifying students as learning disabled. However, as with much of what emerged over the past decade from special educators researching reading, programs and practices designed for a very small and narrowly defined population of special learners have tended to become generalized to all learners.

Consider, for example, the research in reading disabilities around phonics and phonological awareness occurring in the late 1990s. Advocates of early intervention programs based on work with so-called dyslexics found themselves with unimagined leverage to influence reading curriculum and policy in the United States when George W. Bush, a strident supporter of phonics, was elected President. With the institutionalizing of phonics and phonological awareness as national educational policy through the instrument of Reading First, reading programs across the country were compelled to adopt intense skills-based early reading programs for all children, even though the research upon which the methods were derived came from studies with special populations of dyslexic readers (c.f., Foorman, Francis, Fletcher, Schatschneider, & Mehta, 1998; Foorman & Torgesen, 2001). In other words, the science behind the early reading interventions was with seriously disabled readers; yet the methods had to be provided to all students if states and districts hoped to receive federal funding to support reading (Allington, 2008).

This same pattern appears to be repeating itself with RTI, especially at the secondary level. How can IDEA, legislation for the learning disabled, spawn a system of instruction and intervention for struggling and non-struggling students alike? The answer lies in the language of IDEA requiring schools to institute preventive measures that attempt to reduce the number of students who experience initial failure. Within a tiered model of RTI, the frontline of prevention is Tier 1 or the general education classroom. Here is where every student regardless of ability is to receive *high quality* instruction. Furthermore, in an era of limited resources and personnel, secondary schools have not had the luxury to create multiple approaches to delivering reading services, so have tended toward approaches sanctioned by government officials and policymakers controlling reading and special education research and program dollars. As a result, RTI, with the government's seal of approval, has quickly emerged from special education legislation and literature to become a new attractive framework for adolescent literacy in middle and high schools.

CHAPTER SUMMARY

Because RTI has its roots in special education, it is regarded by many as a compensatory program for the reading and learning disabled. However, IDEA stipulates that whichever approach is adopted for addressing the needs of learning disabled students it should be preventive as well as interventive. Furthermore, the approach must have a scientific basis

Although RTI is not specifically identified as the approach of choice in IDEA, it is being touted as a system that will prevent reading and learning difficulties from developing and address those that have developed. The RTI approach typically entails three main components: 1. universal screening of students to determine which level of intervention is appropriate for each, 2. an increasingly focused regimen of interventions designed to prevent or ameliorate reading and learning problems, and 3. frequent evaluation to monitor student progress with targeted instruction.

Two broad areas of critique of RTI for secondary literacy were raised in this chapter. The first has to do with an obvious disconnect between the requirement in IDEA that approaches to dealing with learning disabled students' academic needs be scientifically based and, at the same time, the glaring lack of any evidence—scientific or otherwise—for the efficacy of secondary RTI programs. The second area of critique centered on whether RTI, which emerged from special education literature and legislation, should become the blueprint for a comprehensive literacy program. In the next chapter, I take up this latter issue by exploring the challenges of putting in place an overall reading program in secondary schools based on RTI-like features.

Relate to Integrate

Whether you are working individually or with a group of others, take a few moments to reflect on the chapter that you have just read. To facilitate your learning, consider the following:

1. What are the benefits of RTI as compared to the discrepancy approach of LD identification?

Individual: Make a list of benefits of RTI in contrast to the discrepancy approach to LD identification. Write a journal reflection of the contrasts.

Group: Have participants brainstorm pros and cons of the RTI approach as compared to the discrepancy model. Have facilitator record responses and lead discussion.

2. What are some challenges of RTI at the secondary level?

Individual: What do you see as the most significant challenges that face implementation of an RTI program in a secondary school? List these in your journal and describe how you would overcome these hurdles.

Group: Have participants form small groups. Have each group generate and prioritize a list of the most significant challenges that face implementation of an RTI program in a secondary school. Once groups have completed this activity, have facilitator gather and record responses. Have large group discuss potential solutions to counteract the challenges.

CHAPTER 2

Problems Applying RTI in Literacy at the Secondary Level

HIGHLIGHTS

- American middle and high schools are complex institutions that can limit the feasibility of applying an elementary-level model of RTI at that level.
- Providing responsive literacy instruction to meet the needs of youth with diverse reading and learning abilities presents enormous challenges for advocates of RTI in secondary settings.
- Complexities related to school structure, teaching culture, and adolescent identity will need to be taken into account when planning and implementing an RTI-like system at the secondary level.

IN CHAPTER 1 I asserted that RTI approaches in middle and high school contexts will only be as effective as Tier 1 supports for preventing reading and learning difficulties. Otherwise, RTI at the secondary level becomes little more than a delivery system for remedial reading and, as such, cannot be regarded as a comprehensive program for developing the literacy competencies of all youth.

If RTI is to be regarded as a comprehensive system, then responsive literacy instruction must occur in classrooms throughout the school building and across the disciplines. This means teachers of science, history, math, and language arts should form the frontline of prevention in a successful RTI system. Yet, given the secondary schools we have, our expectations for content area teachers must be tempered by several factors that impinge on their motivation and ability to undertake the challenges of meeting the literacy and learning needs of all their students. These factors include 1. structural conditions, such as rigid departmentalization and complex scheduling schemes; 2. school culture issues related to teacher identity and efficacy; 3. availability of support structures provided by district and school leaders, including comprehensive and sustained commitment, as well as adequate material and professional development resources.

Along with factors and conditions related to school structure and the teaching culture of secondary schools that affect successful implementation of RTI-like systems at that level, we must also give serious consideration to adolescent students themselves, their identities, needs, attitudes, and motivations. As has been established, the unique characteristics of older youth will influence any school-based program or approach that is intended for them (Brozo, 2006a; Cook-Sather, 2002a).

STRUGGLING ADOLESCENT READERS AND RTI

Go back far enough in the history of American schooling, and the phenomenon of struggling adolescent readers did not exist. This is because in those times youth who had limited literacy abilities or could not read at all were either not allowed, could not afford, or chose not to remain in the schools that were available. For most, schooling went no further than the 8th grade. In 1900, for example, of the 15.5 million students attending public schools in the United

States, only 3% attended high school (National Education Summit on High Schools, 2005). Even with the rise of compulsory secondary education in the United States, it was not until the 1940s that high school matriculation rates began to exceed 50% of the eligible adolescent population. Consequently, those students who continued their education in grades 9 through 12 were generally regarded as having superior academic abilities and/or came from families that could afford a nonworking teenage son or daughter. Thus, there wasn't anything like a program for struggling adolescent readers.

Today, all youth, from disparate cultures and with wide ranging ability levels, attend American secondary schools. Meeting the reading and learning needs of this diverse group is the legal mandate and the professional responsibility of all teachers. Indeed, as we've seen, students' right to participate in the regular classroom curriculum is protected by IDEA; and documenting progress of all students, including those who are English learners, students with disabilities, and students from poverty, has been a requirement of the No Child Left Behind (NCLB) Act.

When NCLB was signed into law in 2002, there were what we now must regard as overly-sanguine expectations that a national emphasis on reading at the primary level would bring all children up to an expected level of performance by 3rd grade (McCray, Vaughn, & Neal, 2001). Assuming the best intentions of NCLB, many children have moved through their elementary years with unaddressed or lingering reading needs (Kohn, 2007; Sunderman, Kim, & Orfield, 2005).

At the same time, a number of students who achieve at expected levels in the first 3 years of elementary school experience serious reading challenges after 3rd grade when required to read and learn from a growing volume of informational and disciplinary texts (Brozo & Afflerbach, 2011; Brozo & Simpson, 2007). Furthermore, older youth from outside the United States who enter our middle and high schools without the benefit of early-grade literacy supports may bring with them a host of language and skills issues (Hawkins, 2004; Ruiz-de-Velasco, Fix, & Clewell, 2001). Consequently, as I pointed out in the Introduction, evidence abounds of struggling adolescent readers.

Now, more than ever, secondary schools are under enormous pressure to find ways of improving reading and academic achievement for struggling students. What has made this challenge doubly difficult is that for many years, particularly in the era of NCLB, secondary reading programs have grown increasingly rare in middle, and even more so, in high schools around the United States (Anders, 2002; Vacca, 1998).

Thus, education systems have been scrambling to put in place new programs to meet the reading and learning needs of adolescents. In the absence of developed and refined programs of adolescent literacy along with a history of local knowledge and expertise to design, implement, and administer such programs, a growing number of school leaders are turning to RTI. The fact that schools everywhere are jumping on the RTI bandwagon makes it easier for others to follow suit. But the biggest appeal, the one that ensures federal support for adolescent literacy intervention efforts, at least through IDEA, is that RTI is regarded as a model founded on "scientifically-based" practices and, consequently, enjoys a stamp of approval from the U.S. federal government (http://ies.ed.gov/ncee/wwc/search/?output=xml_no_dtd&client=wwc&site=wwc&q=rti).

As noted in Chapter 1, although research around RTI at the elementary level has been ongoing, studies into the best ways of implementing the process for secondary students are scant (Duffy, n.d.). Nonetheless, in spite of the lack of scientific evidence for secondary-level RTI, numerous middle and high schools across the United States are forging ahead anyway, struggling to make RTI based on the elementary-school context work for older students (Brozo, 2009/2010). In the next section, I take up the problem of designing and attempting to implement elementary-level models of RTI within the complexity of secondary school contexts.

THE COMPLEXITY OF AMERICAN SECONDARY SCHOOLS

To appreciate how complex modern American secondary schools really are, one need only spend a day or two following teachers, students, and administrators as they traverse the maze of physical and cultural spaces of these institutions. Within such environments, promoting change in the ways middle and high school teachers integrate and apply adolescent literacy practices is always a highly complicated and formidable process (Supovitz & Weinbaum, 2008). It is important, therefore, to unpack the conditions and structures of secondary schools in order to understand the significant ways in which they differ from elementary contexts and, consequently, why in spite of its putative successes in earlier grades RTI for adolescent literacy faces enormous hurdles to full implementation.

Indeed, the most serious hurdle is the relative lack of research examining the application of RTI at the secondary level (Mastropieri & Scruggs, 2005; Samuels, 2009). As pointed out in Chapter 1, although RTI approaches have caught fire across the United States, when it comes to implementing the process for students in middle and high school "the flame abruptly fizzles out" (Samuels, 2009, p. 20). Some studies have provided tentative support for the efficacy of various intervention and assessment strategies appropriate for adolescents (e.g., Calhoon & Fuchs, 2003; Paige, 2006; Papalewis, 2004); however, there are no comprehensive or systematic research studies involving the implementation of RTI in practical secondary school settings (Johnson & Smith, 2008). Indeed, case studies of secondary schools attempting to establish RTI-like systems of assessment and intervention suggest multiple challenges not encountered at the elementary level (Mellard, Layland, & Parsons, 2008). Some of the strongest contrasts between elementary and secondary schools presenting RTI enthusiasts with the biggest challenges include differences in organizational structure, shifts in academic focus, and larger nonschool responsibilities for students (Sugai, 2004). Furthermore, fewer secondary-level instructional practices and interventions, even if evidence-based (Sturtevant et al., 2006), do not always enjoy the type of "scientific" support typically invoked for elementary-level interventions (Johnson & Smith, 2008).

The fact is that most students make a major academic transition when they enter middle school in the United States. They must adjust to a new school, a longer school day, moving from classroom to classroom, receiving content instruction from multiple teachers, and keeping up with the demands of increasingly complex assignments that require critical thinking and independent learning skills. Even for students without a history of reading and learning difficulties, this transition alone can bring on declines in achievement and motivation. The challenges for many youth only increase as they move on to American high schools (Neild, 2009). Robert Belfanz (2009) describes the current state of affairs in typical high schools in the United States:

The past 25 years have also seen significant changes. . . . In many high schools, the movement of special education students into the least restrictive environment, the increase in the number of students learning English as the result of immigration, and the formal dismantling of a rigid tracking system have led to much more diverse and heterogeneous classrooms. In urban and increasingly in older suburban communities, as well as low-wealth rural districts, the growing concentration of poverty has further changed the composition of classrooms—bringing in more students who face a host of environmental and individual challenges associated with living in high-poverty neighborhoods and, often, single-parent households. (p. 29)

Belfanz goes on to say:

At the same time, the standards and accountability movement has brought high-stakes testing, district-wide curricula, pacing guides, and instructional coaches all pushing for more homogenized instruction. Especially in grades and subjects that face high-stakes testing, test preparation has become a commonplace and often time-consuming activity. In high schools with numerous low-performing students, reform has become a habitual activity, often accompanied by a high turnover in administrators. (p. 29)

STRUCTURAL CONDITIONS

Typical secondary school structures are dictating and will continue to dictate the extent to which RTI finds full expression at this level. In contrast to most elementary schools in the United States, middle and high schools are structured in ways that leave little room for the kind of flexibility needed to create multiple overlapping tiers of intervention services to students of varying levels of reading ability. Rigid departmentalization of programs and courses as well as complex scheduling schemes to accommodate large numbers of students in both the regular curriculum and extracurricular activities present the most ardent RTI supporters with enormous logistical challenges.

To better understand how these variables play out every day in the professional lives of secondary teachers, consider the two examples that follow. In the first case at Heritage High School the principal's enthusiasm for RTI comes right up against the reality of trying to organize an effective tiered system at his school. In the second example, Green Middle School, a team of devoted school personnel problem solve their way to instituting a set of responsive literacy services to meet the range of students' needs.

Heritage High School

"Antonio" teaches 10th-grade history in this large multicultural suburban school. He has been teaching for 3 years and is working on a master's degree from a local university. He completed one required reading course and no special education courses during his undergraduate training. As a teacher, he has gone to various professional development workshops sponsored by his district and school, but none dealt specifically with reading across the curriculum or successful practices for struggling readers and learners. In addition to one advanced placement class, he has four sections of general education American history. The size of Antonio's classes range from 18 to 32 students.

Antonio's principal has decided to implement RTI in his school. A week before the start of school, the principal attended a district-sponsored workshop conducted by advocates of RTI, which left him convinced that if he could properly institute universal screening, progress monitoring, and a cascading approach to interventions at Heritage High, it would prevent most reading problems from developing or from getting worse, and would ameliorate those that had developed. The principal has limited resources and even less background knowledge of adolescent literacy, so was quick to seize on a recommendation from the workshop providers that RTI can serve as his school's overall reading program.

A month into the school year, the principal invited the RTI presenters to conduct a workshop for his faculty. The presenters attempted to make the case for creating multiple tiers of intervention, depending on students varying levels of reading competence. They described RTI systems at other schools, though their examples come from programs at the elementary level, and urged the Heritage High faculty to plan a way to implement a similar system in their school.

Antonio and his colleagues are somewhat nonplussed by the workshop. Doesn't their school already have a system of supports for struggling learners? Don't those who qualify receive special education services from certified specialists? Aren't many of those students already assimilated into the general education classroom taught by a content teacher and LD teacher team? Why, they wonder, is a new plan necessary to replace a working compensatory program in place already in their school?

Heritage High's principal responded to these questions by emphasizing that RTI will be a comprehensive program designed to prevent most reading and learning problems from developing and provide focused support for those in need so as to maximize their time in general education classroom instruction. Even with these assurances, the principal and his staff come to recognize shortly after the professional development workshop that RTI introduces at least two immense logistical and cultural challenges. The first will be to prepare all teachers at Heritage, not just the English and special education teachers, to deal with the wide-ranging and differentiated reading and learning needs of students. This will be necessary in order to institute a viable preventive component of the program. The second will be creating spaces in the day to provide targeted interventions for students who, in spite of quality classroom instruction, still need Tier 2 and 3 supports.

Antonio and his Heritage High colleagues soon come to realize that preventive action in the secondary RTI program being proposed by their principal must occur primarily in the general education classroom, within the so-called Tier 1. Otherwise, classroom content-area teachers like Antonio may continue to teach to the curriculum standards but not necessarily to the literacy needs of their students, and will continue to rely on special education teachers to deal with the labeled students within and outside their rooms. If this is the net effect, then Antonio's principal does not have an RTI system but the continuation of a preexisting patchwork of remedial and compensatory services already in place in the school.

While Antonio and his fellow teachers were pondering the implications of new and expanded responsibilities for meeting students' reading and learning needs within an RTI system, the counseling office responsible for scheduling had a near total meltdown. After finally reconciling the nightmare that is the beginning of the school year schedule, they were being asked to determine ways of finding time for small group and individualized instruction in Tiers 2 and 3 contexts. Heritage High's daily schedule is structured on the 50-minute period in which students repeat the same class schedule every day. This rigidity makes it especially difficult to set up alternative times and venues for instruction necessary if a tiered approach is to function as RTI advocates propose.

After a couple of months, as administrative injunctions concerning RTI became increasingly muffled, drowned out by the daily exigencies of running a complex institution, and as faculty and student routines took hold, any serious attempt at RTI-like reforms at Heritage High grew increasingly unlikely. RTI continued to come up in faculty meetings, but conversation shifted from "how can we make this happen" to "we're not ready to make this happen." Antonio continued to be dismayed. Although he was reluctant to take on greater responsibility after just 3 years of experience, when he was finally getting a handle on the curriculum and classroom management, he nonetheless was open to expanding his instructional repertoire to include content literacy and differentiation. This new skill set is what he and his colleagues were told they must develop in order to keep as many students as possible in the classroom meeting the reading and learning expectations.

Finally, in December after several discussions with his staff, counselors, and faculty, the principal decided an RTI system as characterized by the workshop advocates, and he envisioned, was too ambitious for Heritage High. Much more advance planning and professional development would be needed to turn the vaunted rhetoric about RTI by the proponents at the district level into a reality at the high school level. Instead, the principal directed each department to draw up a plan for participating in a tiered intervention program that would be taken into consideration as the school moved toward a renewed attempt at implementation of RTI the following school year.

Green Middle School

In contrast to the desultory and ultimately unsuccessful attempt at integrating an RTI system at Heritage High School, Green Middle School had a more profitable experience due in large measure to the leadership of its principal, Melva. Green, a midsize urban school, is comprised of mostly Hispanic-American and African-American students, many of whom have reading levels below their grade placement. Green Middle had failed to make AYP (adequate yearly progress) according to NCLB guidelines for 3 consecutive years before Melva arrived. After 2 years under Melva's leadership, Green had achieved AYP, though she was not satisfied with its progress and made the decision to institute a comprehensive, schoolwide approach to improving the reading ability for all students. At the same time, Melva's assistant superintendent was urging middle and high schools in the district to integrate a tiered intervention system.

Melva met with her special education teachers and reading specialists just after state test scores were made available in April. Earlier that year, she had assigned her staff to explore and propose a range of possible intervention models to consider for implementation the following year. Now, gathering to digest test results, the team discussed the feasibility of the various intervention plans while poring over test scores. Melva had prepared a chart that showed the relationship between students' scores on the state test and their grade point averages. As common sense would dictate, those scoring at or higher than the 50th percentile had the A's and B's; those below the 50th percentile had the C's, D's, and F's. In other words, the better readers were the more successful students. These internal data would be used to bolster the need for all teachers to put a common shoulder to the wheel to help create a vibrant literate culture at Green.

Several viable options for delivering quality reading services to Green's students were put forward, including forming interdisciplinary teams to link language arts with the other content areas; establishing centers in the content classroom for students to engage in needed skill development and to reinforce understanding of critical vocabulary and concepts; and adopting block scheduling. This last recommendation was in response to the need for more flexibility within each class period so that various levels of responsive instruction could be made available to students with wide-ranging abilities.

Melva was intrigued by the block schedule idea for middle school. She had only been familiar with it at the high school level, so wanted more information about its efficacy and record of success with middle-grade students. Melva asked a couple of teachers on the team to research the feasibility of moving to a block schedule at Green, while she dialogued with district personnel about the possibility of making the shift to something like 90-minute class periods staggered across the week, which seemed to be needed for Green to adopt an RTI-like approach.

It was learned that block scheduling has been used in the United States for over 20 years. The original intention was to create opportunities to explore content in greater depth and for increasing student involvement in learning, which is not as possible when the day is carved up into six or seven short periods. A longer class period allows for multiple teaching and learning experiences, including direct instruction and modeling, small-group work, and individual research and project activity. When students are working in groups or individually, the role of the teacher can then shift from disseminator of information, to facilitator and tutor. Melva realized that freedom to provide extra instruction and support to small numbers of students or one-on-one is an essential ingredient of a comprehensive program designed to meet the reading needs of all students.

A whole-school faculty meeting was held to present the proposal for a revised comprehensive reading program for the following year. Melva first shared the findings of the internal analysis of Green Middle students' reading scores and their grades. Teachers had time to digest these results and discuss. Melva also reinforced the need for all teachers to redouble their efforts to help students increase their reading ability because that improvement would likely translate into higher performance in the classroom. So, teachers could have higher achievers in their content classrooms if they invested time supporting students' reading growth.

Melva then made the case for block scheduling to provide structure for giving students extra reading assistance. Initial reactions were guardedly supportive, though some teachers, particularly those who were in the habit of lecturing, wondered how they would fill 90 minutes of time and keep students' attention. Others expressed concern about students forgetting content if only encountered every other day. Melva's warm though demanding disposition (Irvine & Fraser, 1998) made it clear to her teachers that a new scheduling system was needed in order to create the space for all teachers to provide extra instruction to students exhibiting reading difficulties.

Melva detailed three potential scheduling plans with a 90-minute class design (see Figure 2.1). After lengthy discussion within

Figure 2.1. Three RTI Class Schedules

PLAN 1 CLASS STRUCTURE:	**PLAN 2 CLASS STRUCTURE:**
First 30 Minutes	*First 20 Minutes*
• Detailed Review • Instructional Objectives • Teacher-Led Lesson	• Detailed Review • Instructional Objectives • Cooperative Groups
Second 40 Minutes	*Second 40 Minutes*
• Student Small Groups • Project Work • Student Practice • Individual Assistance Centers	• Small Group Projects • Individual Research • Individual Assistance Centers • Student Practice
Last 20 Minutes	*Last 20 Minutes*
• Return to Whole Class • Debriefing with Students and Teacher • Teacher Closure of Lesson • Student Assessment	• Individual Presentations • Group Presentations • Closure of Lesson • Student Assessment

PLAN 3 CLASS STRUCTURE:

First 75 Minutes	*Second 15 Minutes*
• Flexible Groups • Group Projects • Individual Research • Individual Assistance Centers • Student Presentations	• Debriefing Session with Groups • Debriefing with Whole Class • Student Assessment • Preparation for Next Session

grade-level teams and as a whole faculty about the various class structures Melva proposed, Green Middle School teachers came to appreciate the flexibility a 90-minute class period could offer, especially since classroom teachers were going to be asked to provide extra reading assistance to small groups and individual students. Furthermore, the block format would create opportunities for any advanced students to engage in personally relevant readings and pursue unique projects related to course topics and units.

Once agreement was struck among Melva and her teachers on moving to a block schedule the following year, Melva then invited PTA members and any interested parent to join the conversation about this transition. She held several after-school meetings to explain the goals, benefits, and structure of the new scheduling scheme, as well as respond to parents' questions and concerns. With parents solidly on board, Melva was able to make a formal announcement about the plan at the graduation commencement exercise.

Even while teachers and parents were mobilizing behind Melva's scheduling reform plan, intense preparations were already under way for ensuring teachers would be able to take full advantage of the extended class periods to help all students reach their reading potential. Melva knew she would also have to create numerous and extended professional development opportunities that exposed her faculty to and provided guidance in applying high-quality literacy practices for students of wide ability levels. This facet of Green Middle School's RTI-like program will be taken up in the next section.

To summarize, one of the most vexing, ubiquitous, and vastly under researched challenges for proponents of RTI in American middle and high schools is scheduling for tiered interventions. If space cannot be found or created within the school day for deserving students to receive appropriate instructional supports, then the foundation upon which RTI rests—that is, the flexibility to create tiered interventive contexts for students depending upon their responses to the instruction provided within each—is undermined.

The experience of both Heritage High and Green Middle administrators, staff, and faculty remind us that secondary school reforms are fraught with challenges. The daunting structural constraints on the implementation of an RTI-like program proved insuperable for the principal and his colleagues at Heritage High. However, Melva, with her foresight and penchant for consensus building, was able to put responsive teaching structures in place that surmounted barriers of scheduling and traditional classroom instructional delivery.

RTI in the Real World

PORTLAND PUBLIC SCHOOLS STRIVING READERS

Interventions utilize University of Kansas Center for Research on Learning's Strategic Instruction Model (SIM) Content Literacy Curriculum at four high schools and five middle schools in the Portland WA district (grades 7–10). Program consists of both Tier 1 and Tier 2 interventions and each school is staffed with a full-time instructional coach as well as a monthly visit from the Strategic Learning Center (SLC), the organization tasked with oversight of the program. Monthly visits provide additional support to teachers along with site-based training.

Eligibility to participate in the targeted Tier 2 intervention was based on a cutoff score of the OSAT (Oregon Scholastic Aptitude Test) combined with the Degrees of Reading Power (DRP) test. The Year 1 intervention had 275 participants, and in Year 2 that number expanded to 350. Students who exceeded the cutoff scores in the nine participating middle and high schools became subjects in the Tier 1 intervention, approximately 700 to 800 students per year.

Tier 1. The Tier 1 intervention program integrated all parts of their curricula with Content Enhancement Routines (CERs) with the help of GIST software to present material in organized, understandable charts that clearly identify learning objectives. Language arts and social studies teachers received training for Year 1 of the program, followed by math and science teachers in Year 2, and other subject areas (ESL, P.E. special education, etc.) will be trained in Year 3. Initial professional development for each teacher consists of approximately 55 hours of training run by SLC, followed by a variable amount of training over the remaining years to be determined by each school's administrators.

Measure of Student Reading Outcomes: Oregon State Assessment Test (OSAT)

Tier 2. The Tier 2 intervention model was Xtreme Reading, developed by the University of Kansas Center for Research on Learning's Strategic Instruction Model (SIM). This program stresses seven areas of literacy instruction: Vocabulary, Word Mapping, Visual

Imagery, Self-Questioning, Inference, Paraphrasing, and LINCing. Teaching methods taught in professional development include teacher modeling, direct instruction, paired student practice, and independent practice. Each unit includes an assessment to track student progress over one year of participation. Although reading specialists and content teachers paired up to teach these intervention classes for Years 1 and 2 of the program, Year 3 was modified so that only one trained intervention teacher took control of the intervention classes.

Measures of Student Reading Outcomes: Oregon State Assessment Test (OSAT) and Group Reading Assessment and Diagnostic Evaluation (GRADE)

CRITICAL QUESTIONS:

The Portland Public Schools Striving Readers program includes only two tiers of intervention. Think about what a third tier of intervention might look like for students who need individual literacy interventions.

- How would this be assessed?
- Where could this fit into the existing tiered structure?
- What kind of specific interventions may be appropriate?
- How would progress be monitored?
- Who would provide these interventions?
- What structural supports are necessary to make Tier 2 interventions possible in Portland?

SCHOOL CULTURE AND TEACHER IDENTITY

It has been established that the culture of secondary schools (O'Brien, Stewart, & Moje, 1995) imposes limits on the feasibility of RTI as a comprehensive model of reading at that level. In elementary-level, self-contained classrooms, a teacher may have a single group of students the entire day. Providing whole-class, small-group, and individualized reading instruction is not only possible within that setting but an expectation. Additionally, weaving the language arts into all aspects of the curriculum is readily achieved in typical early grades' classrooms.

In contrast, consider someone like Antonio, the 10th-grade American history teacher at Heritage High. He sees a group of students each day for 48 minutes, is under strong pressure to cover the content standards and grade-level expectancies of American history, and is only superficially knowledgeable of and less experienced in content literacy strategies. Furthermore, based on my experience, teachers like Antonio are apt to see themselves first and foremost as specialists in content, which they impart through whole group lessons, and provide help to individual students who seek it over that same content. Students who need extra literacy and learning supports are referred by Antonio and his colleagues to other high school specialists, such as the reading and special education teacher.

In middle and high schools, prevention of literacy and learning difficulties in the RTI sense means the best possible instruction in content area classrooms. Yet, those of us well-seasoned in school-based, adolescent literacy reform know how difficult it is to overcome resistance by middle and high school teachers to incorporate responsive literacy practices into their daily lessons (Brozo & Simpson, 2007; Plaut, 2009). Thus, RTI's most important first tier is its weakest link at the secondary level. If responsive literacy instruction isn't provided at Tier 1, many students who might otherwise be able to succeed without Tier 2 or 3 interventions—and avoid the time, attention, and stigma often associated with remedial instruction—will inevitably find themselves in need of intensive remediation. In other words, RTI at the secondary level is only as good as its preventive supports. In the end, if secondary classroom teachers fail to offer responsive literacy instruction to benefit every student and differentiated assistance for those in need of extra help, then the preventive potential of RTI is lost.

Traditionally, in secondary schools across the United States, students' literacy development has been seen as the English teacher's responsibility (Alger, 2007). This has remained largely the case, in spite of numerous calls over the past decade for an increased emphasis on developing literacy within all classrooms (c.f., Biancarosa & Snow, 2004; Draper, 2008). Schoolwide responsibility for literacy is thought to benefit students, who would not only expand reading, writing, and critical thinking abilities in disciplinary classrooms but also use those abilities to enrich disciplinary knowledge (Brozo, 2010b; Fisher & Ivey, 2005; Moje, 2008).

In spite of over 100 years of accumulated knowledge about secondary literacy (Mraz, Rickelman, & Vacca, 2009) and the exhortations of scholars, many middle and high school administrators fail to make literacy teaching across the curriculum a priority and, consequently, teachers continue to make little room for literacy instruction in the content classroom (Draper, Smith, Hall, & Sieber, 2005; Hall, 2005; Lester, 2000). Explanations for the failure of secondary teachers to accommodate literacy in their daily instruction have included the cultural values of teachers and students, the structures of secondary schools, and the dominance of curricular norms (Alvermann & Moore, 1991; Moore, 1996; O'Brien, Stewart, & Moje, 1995).

To be sure, when secondary school culture is examined, it's impossible to overlook what Donahue (2003) identifies as "disciplinary divides." This mindset pervades middle and high schools and reinforces teaching as the transmission of content. It also brings teachers to the view that reading and writing skills should have been developed in primary and elementary grades (Greenleaf, Schoenbach, Cziko, & Mueller, 2001; McCoss-Yergian & Krepps, 2010). Although disciplinary expertise is an essential attribute of a quality secondary-level teacher, it can be an impediment to the realization of RTI at the secondary level, which requires all teachers, regardless of what they teach and the context of instruction, to contribute to the leavening of students' literacy competencies. For reasons stated already, this responsibility is especially critical in typical content classrooms with mixed abilities, because of the expressed goal of RTI to prevent reading and learning problems from developing in Tier 1 environments. Prevention of student reading and learning difficulties in secondary classrooms will only be possible if all teachers are highly trained in effective literacy practices for supporting meaning making of disciplinary text and meeting the needs of diverse learners.

SUPPORT STRUCTURES

Another critical consideration as to why secondary teachers can be resistant to the idea that a collective effort is needed to elevate the reading and writing abilities of youth is whether they have received appropriate training and developed effective skills in adolescent literacy (Brozo, 2009/2010). Further complicating RTI-like reforms at the middle and high school levels is that teachers in the content areas can be identified as highly qualified according to NCLB standards while lacking any meaningful training in reading and writing instruction needed to address the literacy challenges of a growing number of adolescents (Langer, 2004).

No secondary teacher should be considered highly qualified if lacking the knowledge and ability to meet the range of reading and writing needs adolescent students present. As I have discovered in my own school reform projects, without additional professional development, secondary-level teachers may never gain the proper tools to enhance reading achievement and expand disciplinary knowledge for youth. Therefore, an efficacious program of professional development must be the heart of any reform effort intended to help all adolescents maximize their literacy and learning potential.

When secondary teachers lack understanding of responsive literacy practices to make disciplinary text accessible to all, even normally developing students are susceptible to reading difficulties. However, those already struggling readers and learners may be especially vulnerable (Brozo & Simpson, 2007). There are numerous indications that youth of color (Tatum, 2008; Jiménez & Teague, 2007) and those receiving special education services (Fisher, Schumaker, & Deshler, 2002) are not getting adequate training in higher-level literacy skills (Biancarosa & Snow, 2004; Braunger, Donahue, Evans, & Galguera, 2005). Nevertheless, these students can be taught to improve their reading and thinking abilities when appropriate strategies are adapted to meet their unique learning needs (Brozo & Puckett, 2009; Greenleaf, Jimenez, & Roller, 2002). Equally significant is the finding that secondary teachers can develop self-efficacy as content literacy teachers through appropriate coaching and professional development (Cantrell & Hughes, 2008; Park & Osborne, 2006).

To make vivid the indispensable nature of quality professional development for ensuring the establishments of a genuinely effective RTI system, let's return to Heritage High and Green Middle schools.

Heritage High School

As we saw, Heritage High was unable to launch RTI in the first year, as the principal had hoped, because of insurmountable problems with scheduling for tiered interventions. But this was only the beginning of their challenges with turning the principal's goal of a schoolwide RTI program into reality. Lurking behind the logistics of such an initiative was the entrenched "disciplinary divide" culture of Heritage High's faculty. Transforming attitudes and skill sets to accommodate the preventive and interventive practices of RTI would require resources beyond those available to the principal.

The principal made an initial attempt to bring his faculty up to speed with the nature of the RTI reforms he desired by sponsoring a PD session by the same district facilitators he had seen present. The presentation left some teachers like Antonio unsure about the new expectations he and his colleagues would have to assume. Other teachers were vocal in their resistance to the idea that an RTI system could be put in place that year. The principal and his assistants came to the same realization, so decided to try rekindling interest in the initiative before the start of the following school year.

When Heritage High teachers reported during the week prior to the arrival of students and the official start of classes, they were required to attend a full workshop day devoted to RTI. The national speaker gave a rousing pep talk on the merits and potential benefits of an RTI system for Heritage. The faculty was given suggestions for using existing test data for universal screening purposes, turning everyday texts into progress monitoring tools, and whole, small-group, and individual teaching strategies for students with varying literacy and learning needs. Teachers were polite, asked relevant questions, and participated actively in the session. When the speaker concluded, the principal took the podium to say that each department would have a copy of the speaker's book, and he expected a specific plan for implementing an RTI system by the end of September.

As informative and useful as the workshop may have been, the future of RTI at Heritage High School would not be bright. This is because there were few if any provisions for follow-up PD on the topic or support staff with knowledge of and experience with RTI at the secondary level to provide ongoing technical assistance to teachers. The complexity of tiered interventions, as we have seen, requires orchestration of teachers and resources in ways that challenge the structure and culture of secondary schools like Heritage High. Antonio, the young history teacher, was feeling especially challenged as he left the RTI workshop. The pressure on general education classroom teachers like him seemed enormous, as they were expected to address the reading needs of every student in his class in order to limit the number who might qualify for small-group and/or individual interventions.

Like the previous year, it wasn't long before Heritage High teachers and administrators shifted their priorities to the myriad daily exigencies that come with the start of a new academic year. By the end of September, the due date for an RTI plan was pushed back another month. These delays continued. Most teachers engaged in a kind of passive resistance to the principal's goal for an RTI program by commiserating privately about their reservations while failing to make any changes in their instructional approaches and offering explanations of appeasement to assistant principals when they showed up at department meetings. By the midyear holidays, it seemed another year would pass without much if any action on the principal's hope for an RTI-like reading program at Heritage High School. By February, the school focus shifted once more to upcoming state testing in early April. Talk of RTI all but died during those two months.

Finally, after testing in late April, at a whole-school faculty meeting, the principal renewed his call for RTI plans from each department. Shortly afterward, assistant principals (APs) met with departments to check on progress of the plans. It was there the passive resistance spilled out into full-fledged push-back. Teachers in every department, including English, gave the APs an earful about the lack of ongoing support and resources needed to implement a realistic RTI system. High on the list of complaints was that classroom teachers didn't have the skills or the time to teach reading, as their curriculum was already packed with content impossible to cover in 48-minute periods and in time for annual testing.

Green Middle School

Melva's successful push to reform the class schedule at Green Middle set the stage for a comprehensive, schoolwide literacy program. As pleased with this development as they were, Melva and her team had been working on a parallel track to gaining approval for block scheduling that would set into motion a professional development plan designed to expand her teachers' knowledge and skills related to disciplinary literacy and literacy practices for struggling readers. She understood that if responsive literacy instruction was to occur at Green, teachers would need not only time but also expertise.

Virtually all secondary reading programs with demonstrated effectiveness attribute comprehensive staff development as an essential ingredient of success (Brozo & Fisher, 2010; Sturtevant et al., 2006). RTI-like reforms that require teachers to deliver responsive literacy instruction schoolwide are likely to take hold when teachers are provided extensive teacher professional development.

Melva knew building expertise in literacy practices among her staff would require consistent effort over time. It would need to be done in collaboration with faculty and not something done to them. And it would demand much more than just one or two workshops to reach the desired goal of maximizing prevention of student reading problems and making available targeted supports for all students who exhibit a need for them.

With the support of district administration, Melva and her team researched and devised a plan with the goal of imbuing every teacher with confidence to meet the reading and learning needs of all Green Middle's students. The PD plan was structured around the following three guidelines: 1. offer teachers a manageable and realistic number of new literacy practices; 2. guide teachers in the classroom as they apply new literacy practices taken from workshops; and 3. establish forums for teachers to inform and refine PD initiatives.

Offer teachers a manageable and realistic number of new strategies. The overarching goal of Green Middle School's PD plan was to ensure every teacher was taking equal responsibility for the literacy growth of all students. To gain needed skills to meet this expectation, teachers would need scaffolding for change just as their students would. Melva and her team knew if, overwhelmed by a large number of new adolescent literacy strategies, teachers may find it easier to stick with the status quo than try to decide which strategies to apply.

Melva, therefore, invited her teachers to agree upon a set number of initiatives they were all willing to embrace that first year. In this way she hoped to provide consistency for students and a common set of schoolwide literacy instructional practices with which teachers could develop expertise. A commitment to a smaller but more manageable set of practices at Green Middle helped teachers feel as though everyone was putting a common shoulder to the wheel in advancing the literacy reforms.

Guide teachers in the classroom as they apply new literacy practices taken from workshops. In-service workshops are the most common form of professional development for middle and high school faculty implementing new literacy initiatives. They provide teachers "first exposure" (Cooter, 2004) to particular approaches but not the capacity to apply them in actual instructional contexts. Consequently, one or two workshops alone rarely bring about lasting change or "deep learning" (Cooter, 2004), unless coupled with provisions for supporting teachers' sustained efforts to implement literacy and learning innovations (Langer, 2004).

Not as common are in-class teaching demonstrations conducted by a workshop leader or consultant. At Green Middle, Melva provided two full-day workshops just before the start of the new school year, and then had the reading coach and lead teachers go into colleagues' classrooms throughout the year to conduct lessons using the strategies demonstrated in the workshops. This was followed up with opportunities for teachers to team-teach the strategies or try them on their own with peer feedback.

Establish forums for teachers to inform and refine PD initiatives. Melva and her team knew that their teachers not only needed to acquire knowledge of new adolescent literacy practices, but also needed to change beliefs about their roles in supporting students' literacy growth. Transforming practices and beliefs requires forums be established for teachers to have a genuine voice in planning, implementing, and evaluating reforms. At Green Middle, teachers gathered in focus groups to discuss and propose literacy priorities for their students.

In addition, Melva formed a staff development committee responsible for identifying PD priorities among the staff and finding appropriate in-service workshop facilitators to ensure these priorities were being addressed. The committee, with Melva's support, provided additional monthly meetings to allow teachers to discuss their challenges and successes with the new literacy practices. These meetings were held during the school day to ensure maximum attendance and participation as well as to embed professional development into the school day.

In sum, we see once again two contrasting scenes of secondary school reform around RTI. At Heritage High, like many U.S. high schools, there is reluctance on the part of content-area teachers to commit to including literacy as a goal. The literacy needs of students are often viewed as someone else's responsibility by disciplinary teachers like Antonio and his colleagues. This often results in classroom teachers covering content without regard for the literacy skills students must possess to read and write about this content. RTI systems, however, demand that all teachers are prepared to deliver high-quality literacy instruction to each of their students. The PD approach at Heritage High to prepare Antonio and the rest of the faculty for this responsibility was far from adequate, resulting in resistance to RTI-like reforms and a failed attempt to implement RTI in the second year.

Melva's PD approach at Green Middle, on the other hand, ensured maximum buy-in from her teachers, administrators, and even parents to a comprehensive and responsive literacy program intended to address the reading needs of every student.

THE COMPLEXITY OF ADOLESCENCE

Secondary schools are honeycombed with various cultures, discourse communities, and stakeholders that have direct and indirect effects on reform initiatives. Perhaps, one of the most potent of these influences on the success or failure of reform activities are the students themselves (Brozo, 2006a).

Adolescence as a stage of development represents another clear demarcation of difference between elementary and secondary school contexts. Young children are more likely to be compliant when their teachers introduce new or different instructional practices. They are more likely to behave in ways that please their teachers rather than conform to peer expectations. In short, they are not yet engaged in the active and self-conscious process of identity construction that marks adolescence (Erikson, 1980; Gee, 2001; McCarthey & Moje, 2002).

By contrast, at the middle school level a well-documented slump in school engagement occurs (Anderman, Maehr, & Midgley, 1999;

Eccles, Lord, & Buchanan, 1996; Gottfried, Fleming, & Gottfried, 2001; Guthrie & Davis, 2003). This decline in students' academic interest can persist through high school (Board on Children, Youth, and Families, 2003; Cappella & Weinstein, 2001; Neild, Stoner-Eby, Furstenburg, 2008). Biancarosa and Snow (2004) expressed the concern that it is more difficult to improve adolescent reading achievement than it is in elementary school because "adolescents are not as universally motivated to read better or as interested in school-based reading" (p. 2).

Thus, efforts by enthusiastic, reform-minded administrators and teachers may meet with limited success if adolescent students are not equally enthusiastic about these reforms. In other words, the ways in which adolescent students take up any new initiatives will determine their success.

To situate RTI-like reforms in secondary contexts, consider how adolescents' level of willingness to be complicit in classroom-content literacy practices, regular testing for progress monitoring, intervention work in small-groups, and one-on-one tutorials will impact the effectiveness of these activities. If youth perceive RTI initiatives as unrelated to their goals, interests, and needs they may exert less effort, resulting in little changes in achievement. If, on the other hand, adolescents find RTI-like literacy supports appealing and relevant to their needs as readers and learners, then they are more likely to benefit from them by increasing achievement (Conley & Hinchman, 2004; Kamil, Borman, Dole, Kral, Salinger, & Torgesen, 2008).

The educational change literature (Fullan, 2007) while making vivid the importance of teachers, school culture, and structural variables in the change process have tended to ignore the effects of and responses to reform initiatives by students. What we have learned is that the relative success or failure of reform efforts will depend to one degree or another on the cooperation and investment of students (Cook-Sather, 2002a). Furthermore, adolescents, like their teachers though unlike most young children, are not compliant functionaries, but critical negotiators of change (Cook-Sather, 2002b) and, thus, should be made to feel a part of a school reform community. Otherwise, the more student voices are muted or silenced in the conversation about school reform, the less likely reform initiatives will be successful (Brozo, 2006a).

Secondary school life is a complex world where participants are in a perpetual state of discourse negotiation (Gee, 2000).

Cook-Sather (2002b) reminds us that within this environment the perspectives most directly affected by, but least often consulted about educational policy, practice, and reform are students. Many have claimed that authorizing students' perspectives can directly improve educational practice by helping teachers better appreciate the lifeworlds of youth and make their teaching more responsive to the experiences and perspectives of students (Cook-Sather, 2002b, 2002c, 2003; Lee, 1999; Wasley, Hampel, & Clark, 1997). Furthermore, when students are taken seriously as knowledgeable members of a reform community, they feel empowered and motivated to participate constructively in their education (Corbett & Wilson, 1995; Heshusius, 1995; Shultz & Cook-Sather, 2001).

RTI-like reforms as conceived by most advocates do not have their genesis in a shared process of development by teachers and students; however that potential exists. RTI is premised on the idea that the more responsive the instructional intervention is to a particular student's reading and learning needs, the greater the likelihood that student will demonstrate growth. Making instruction responsive at the secondary level means listening to adolescents, who unlike their much younger peers in primary and elementary school, are often quite capable of articulating their needs and what might be done to help them (Brozo, 2006a; Lee, 1999). As Cook-Sather (2002a) reminds us, listening to students doesn't always mean doing exactly as they wish, "but it does mean being open to the possibility of revision, both of thought and action" (p. 8). This open approach may help youth think metacognitively and critically about their educational experiences and feel invested in their own learning.

Were concerns for student voice and engagement in RTI reform activity taken into account at either Heritage High or Green Middle schools? When Melva assumed the position of principal at Green Middle she reinvigorated the student council. As with most student councils, Green's was charged with liaising between students and the school administration. However, Melva took pains to ensure student input was not ceremonial but could be incorporated into the idea generation and planning process of the school. She invited council members to participate in conversations about virtually any changes in policy, procedure, and curriculum that would impact students. It was no different with her idea for remaking Green's daily schedule and implementing a comprehensive literacy program. For example, the council also offered suggestions for library and classroom reading materials that would be appealing to the middle graders to increase participation in a planned sustained silent reading (SSR). In addition, with student council members' input, Melva and her team worked out how to make room for SSR during daily homeroom time.

As for Heritage High, unfortunately, the principal failed to build consensus with his faculty, let alone with students, for his desired RTI-like reforms. It is difficult to imagine a student body becoming enthusiastic over the proposed curricular changes at Heritage if their teachers themselves couldn't exhibit enthusiasm for an RTI system.

CHAPTER SUMMARY

Even though RTI has been well studied at the elementary level (Fuchs & Fuchs, 2006) and there are models of what RTI could look like for young children, there is little research on and few examples of how best to implement the process for older students in middle and high school (Cobb, Sample, Alwell, & Johns, 2005; Johnson & Smith, 2008). Thus, in spite of the assumed scientific basis for RTI programs, there is scant evidence to guide secondary schools in the implementation of tiered literacy interventions for upper grades students. This significant lack of research and practical models alone should be enough to give pause to those evidence-minded secondary teachers and administrators. Nevertheless, many schools are forging ahead anyway, struggling to make RTI-like systems work for older students (Goetze, Laster, & Ehren, 2010).

It's clear that secondary classrooms and schools as potential contexts for RTI-like systems are vastly more complex spaces than their primary- and elementary-level counterparts. Factors related to class scheduling, teachers' beliefs and attitudes toward adolescent literacy as well as their perceived areas of expertise, administrative resources and supports, and youth culture and identity will all impinge on the success or failure of programs intended to make responsive literacy instruction available to all. Efforts that ignore these critical factors and attempt to install RTI-like reforms in secondary schools using an elementary model of RTI are destined for disappointment, much like the disappointment experienced by the principal of Heritage High School. If, on the other hand, these factors are honestly and responsibly accounted for in secondary school reform initiatives, as Melva at Green Middle School tried to do, responsive literacy for all has a much better chance of being realized. Realistic and viable approaches to RTI for secondary literacy will be taken up in the next chapter.

Relate to Integrate

Whether you are working individually or with a group of others, take a few moments to reflect on the chapter that you have just read. To facilitate your learning, consider the following:

1. Highlight the differences between the Heritage High School and Green Middle School approaches to implementing RTI.

Individual: Rewrite the Heritage High school scenario, including some of the successful strategies which were employed by Green Middle School.

Group: As a group, revisit the Heritage High school scenario. Discuss how Heritage could have succeeded by using some of the successful strategies that were employed by Green Middle School. Facilitator will lead discussion.

2. How does the concept of the disciplinary divide impact literacy instruction in secondary schools?

Individual: List some ways in which you think that the disciplinary divide impedes literacy instruction in secondary schools? What are some resolutions?

Group: Divide into small groups and discuss the ways in which the disciplinary divide impedes literacy instruction in your school. Prioritize your list and discuss resolutions to your top three items. Facilitator will lead group share out session.

CHAPTER 3

Reframing RTI as Responsive Literacy Instruction for All Adolescent Readers

RESPONSE TO INTERVENTION OR RESPONSIVE INSTRUCTION?

GIVEN RTI's ROOTS, it is important to consider whether an approach to adolescent literacy based on a learning disabilities model is optimum. In this book I have argued for a reconsideration of RTI not strictly as a compensatory model of interventions but as a comprehensive model of adolescent literacy premised on offering responsive instruction to all students.

Moving from a fixed mindset about RTI—as a single model with assumed features that has a long history of positive research and

HIGHLIGHTS

- When RTI is reframed as responsive literacy instruction for all, a comprehensive literacy program can be achievable in secondary school contexts.
- Responsive literacy instruction should be founded on evidence-based principles.
- Responsive literacy instruction looks like different things to different students depending on their abilities, interests, and cultures.
- Responsive literacy instruction at the secondary level must occur first and foremost in the content classroom.
- Responsive literacy instruction at the secondary level is as much about prevention as it is about intervention.

practical success—to a reconception of RTI as responsive literacy instruction requires a small but important shift in thinking. Let's be clear, at its heart RTI is an honorable idea conceived by dedicated professionals to ensure struggling learners get the most effective interventions for increasing learning. All of us can wholeheartedly endorse this critical overarching goal of RTI. What I want to offer is a revisioning of RTI, not a goal shift. My revisioning takes services typically advocated by RTI enthusiasts, such as universal screening, tiered interventions, and progress monitoring, and redeliver them in the form of low-stakes schoolwide testing, responsive/differentiated literacy instruction, and formative assessment conducted by teachers as well as students in the form of self-assessment.

Furthermore, consider the significance of the subtle but powerful shift in terminology from intervention to responsive instruction in my revisioning of RTI. The word *intervention* as used in the context of behavioral health refers to a process that has the effect of modifying an individual's behavior, cognition, or emotional state. Because the field of learning disabilities has strong roots in behaviorism, a nomenclature has built up around LD practices that is distinctly clinical, with treatments for learning difficulties administered in ways not unlike a medical professional's prescriptions. Whether this deficit model has a place at all in adolescent literacy programs has been justifiably challenged (Alvermann, 2003; Moje, 2002; O'Brien, 2001); nonetheless, however applicable it might be to some, it breaks down when applied to all learners and when prevention is a paramount goal.

I have elected, therefore, to use *responsive instruction* instead of *intervention* as a more inclusive expression for approaches that ensure all students receive the best possible literacy supports within a comprehensive program in secondary schools. I have done this because like all terms and labels, once embedded in the professional vernacular they have a way of reifying expectations and practices for students (Brozo & Simpson, 2007; Polakow & Brozo, 1994). Think of it this way, if a 7th-grader of color from a single-parent household in poverty who is a recent immigrant receives unresponsive instruction because the school he attends employs teachers ill-prepared to deal with his literacy and language needs, then failure and interventions may be inevitable (Brozo & Brozo, 1994). Alternatively, if the 7th-grader's teachers regard such a youth as a resource with multilingual and multicultural flexibility and the potential to make great strides given quality instruction, then reading and learning difficulties and remedial measures may not be predestined (Brozo, 1995; Brozo, 1990).

Thus, if a label must exist, I endorse responsive *instruction* over *intervention*, since the latter implies deficit, deficiency, or handicap. This is not because I fail to appreciate the challenges youth who need further development in literacy pose, but to urge a different set of expectations and practices based on language that describes youth in a way that values the strengths they possess, their effort, and potential.

Another important terminological issue has to do with how to characterize RTI. It has been convincingly argued that RTI is not a formal program but just one of many possible approaches that attempts to respond to calls in IDEA for dealing with students learning difficulties (Allington, 2008; Scanlon & Anderson, 2010). Some RTI advocates, however, have urged the use of formal and commercially prepared products for screening, providing tiered interventions, and progress monitoring, as though these components are codified in the Act. In this book, the word *program* will not be made in connection with RTI. Other words, such as *approach* or *RTI-like reforms*, will be used instead. When the word *program* is used it will be made in reference to a coordinated, comprehensive array of services and practices to develop the various literacies adolescents need to be successful in secondary schools. In this sense, I will not have any particular formal or commercial program in mind.

ENVISIONMENTS OF
RESPONSIVE LITERACY INSTRUCTION

Let's consider, then, what instruction looks like when it meets the needs of individual adolescent readers and learners. In other words, let's envision responsive instruction.

Matt. Matt is an intelligent 9th-grader with little motivation to read school texts. Anthony, an observant science teacher, takes note of Matt's disengagement and checks his records. Anthony discovers Matt was an "A" student in 8th grade, with high test scores in reading. He meets with Matt to hear from Matt himself about what he thinks is interfering with his reading. Matt tells Anthony reading the science texts bores him, they make him sleepy, and because his mind wanders, he often fails to understand what he reads. Anthony probes further by asking Matt what he thinks would help him become more motivated to read in science class. Matt responds by saying he knows he's a good reader because when he reads on topics of interest, he "totally gets it." Matt goes on to tell his science teacher that he spends much of his free time skateboarding with his friends, playing computer and video games, and reading graphic novels. Armed with this information, Anthony creates Webquests for Matt to read and gather information about scientific topics from interesting Internet sites. For example, when studying Newtonian laws of physics, Matt is directed to the site, "Skateboard Science" (http://myexploratorium.org/skateboarding/index.html) to explore how these physical principles apply to his favorite sport. Matt creates a multimedia presentation on the topic, including narration over video clips of his own dare devil tricks.

This is responsive literacy instruction because Anthony met Matt where he was motivationally, and engendered a heightened level of engagement and an increase in comprehension through the use of alternatives to traditional print text.

Deeqa. Deeqa, a recent immigrant from Somalia, enters Eva's 8th-grade social studies classroom with limited English proficiency. Her limited knowledge of English is compounded by the increasing demand on middle-grade students to read and understand complex text and the academic vocabulary in books and other readings in the subject areas. As a consequence, Deeqa is struggling to keep up. Eva's experience with students from a range of language and cultural backgrounds made it easier to recognize Deeqa's reading and learning challenges, and she quickly employed support activities to ease her transition. Eva has learned that it is critical for all her students, but especially those who are struggling to learn English, to be given frequent opportunities for sustained encounters with diverse texts. Eva set aside 20 minutes of each 90-minute class block for independent silent reading on social studies topics, such as researching a country of their ethnic heritage. Deeqa and the rest of the class were allowed to self-select print materials from the school's and her classroom library, access the Internet for interesting things to read, or read texts they brought to class. During this time, Eva helped Deeqa find reading material that was appropriate to her abilities, interesting, and culturally relevant, which included books and magazines from home in the Somali language that Deeqa translated, as well sources they found on the Internet. Eva assisted Deeqa as needed, helping her with vocabulary, encouraging her to read certain passages multiple times, modeling fluent reading, and asking questions to promote understanding. Eva also sought ideas and support from Deeqa's ESOL (English for Speakers of Other Languages) teacher, who suggested pairing Deeqa with an 8th-grade Somali girl, Ayanna, who had developed proficiency with reading, writing, and speaking English. Arrangements were made with Ayanna's teacher to read and write with Eva during the 20 minutes of time set aside for this activity in Eva's class.

This is responsive literacy instruction because Deeqa's social studies teacher made space in her classroom for Deeqa to have regular and sustained experiences with accessible print and digital sources to increase her English language proficiency. In addition, Eva and another student provided needed individual reading and writing assistance to Deeqa.

Donelle. Donelle, a 10th-grader with a reading level of 8th grade, receives reading support in his English class within the context of daily activities and lessons. And Donelle is not alone; several of his classmates also bring reading abilities to the English class that are not commensurate with their grade level. Ruby, his teacher, never assumes all of her students can handle the challenging poems, essays, stories, and plays in the literature anthology without assistance, so she employs a reciprocal reading approach. As each piece is read and discussed, Ruby embeds in her instruction explicit modeling of four essential comprehension processes: predicting, questioning, clarifying, and summarizing. After demonstrating predicting, she encourages Donelle and the other students to practice making predictions about text themselves. Eventually, over time, after Ruby has repeatedly demonstrated and elicited from students the four comprehension processes, she forms several groups of four students and directs each student in the group takes responsibility for one of the four comprehension processes. Ruby moves throughout the room, monitoring groups as they progress through a section of text by making and checking predictions, asking questions, seeking clarification to confusing or unresolved aspects of the text, and finally summarizing what they read.

This is responsive literacy instruction because Donelle and the other students are receiving literacy supports within the English classroom. Their teacher, Ruby, doesn't wait for students to fail but mediates understanding of the anthologized readings by modeling and eliciting critical comprehension processes. Because Donelle and his classmates are provided guided practice in applying these processes on their own, they're developing independent literacy skills needed for reading any complex text.

In these three cases several critical principles of responsive literacy instruction are at play. These principles can serve as guides to those designing and delivering comprehensive adolescent literacy programs that seek to respond to each student's literacy and learning needs with responsive instruction.

Principle 1: Responsive Literacy Instruction Views Adolescents as a Resource

The perspectives most directly affected by, but least often consulted about educational practice, are students (Cook-Sather, 2002a). I discovered this to be true in my own investigation of students' perceptions of a high school's new reading program (Brozo, 2006a). Interviews of a cross-section of the student body, including striving readers, revealed that youth are often mindful of how they are discounted when new initiatives are planned and implemented. As a result, the students were not motivated to contribute to the success of new schoolwide literacy program. Indeed, end-of-year state test results for the school proved disappointing in spite of the reforms as achievement levels were essentially flat in reading. I concluded that the school might have found more responsive and effective approaches to improving reading and content learning if the students, for whom the initiatives were intended, had been allowed to give input before and all throughout the year.

To invite striving readers and all students into an open dialog about what they need to become more engaged and increase competence requires viewing them as resources (Brozo, 2006b; Gutierrez, Morales, & Martinez, 2009). Many have shown how students' perspectives can directly improve educational practice by helping teachers better appreciate the lifeworlds of youth and make their teaching more responsive to the experiences and attitudes of students (Cook-Sather, 2002a, 2002b, 2003; Lee, 1999; Wasley, Hampel, & Clark, 1997). Furthermore, when students are taken seriously as a resource, they feel empowered and motivated to participate constructively in their education (Corbett & Wilson, 1995; Heshusius, 1995; Shultz & Cook-Sather, 2001).

Obtaining the input from struggling readers on how to make teaching more responsive to their needs is not a feature of RTI, even though this could provide teachers insights not possible through traditional assessment means. Lee (1999), for example, demonstrated that high school striving readers can be informants to help bring about curricular reforms that support responsive literacy practices. The struggling readers he worked with were quite capable of articulating the nature of their learning problems and offering legitimate recommendations for instructional modifications to teachers and administrators.

Teachers who value the unique identities of each adolescent will find ways of making reading and learning experiences personally meaningful and culturally responsive (Moje, 2002). They recognize the important contributions each student can make to the construction of knowledge and development of literacy in the classroom. More significantly, their practices buoy self-efficacy especially for striving readers with a history of learning failure by valuing their ideas, attitudes, and experiences.

Secondary teachers who take advantage of their students as resources structure numerous opportunities for youth to bring to the learning context their store of knowledge and experiences (Moje, McIntosh Ciechanowski, Kramer, Ellis, Carrillo, & Collazo, 2004). Teachers use these funds of knowledge their students possess to inform selection of text for practicing strategies and developing skills, as well as for recreational reading. They know that making meaning through reading and writing depends on students' individual perceptions that can be enhanced through interaction and collaboration (Brozo & Simpson, 2007).

Furthermore, when students' voices regarding curricular content and demonstrations of accomplishment are genuinely considered, the relevancy and meaningfulness of academic literacy and learning are reinforced (Bomer, 1999). When striving readers see that their input is valued because it helped reshape someone else's perceptions and attitudes about a text passage, piece of writing, video, or class activity, their self-efficacy as readers and learners expands.

Principle 2: Responsive Literacy Instruction Occurs Within Comprehensive Literacy Programs

Middle and high school classroom teachers have always recognized that adolescents who encounter difficulties learning can usually attribute their frustrations to major shortcomings in their reading ability (Hock & Deshler, 2003). This means that as students' reading achievement increases so does their performance in all the subject areas. The relationship between reading scores and overall grade point average has been well documented in findings from the National Assessment of Educational Progress (Donahue, Daane, & Grigg, 2003). Thus, all teachers regardless of their disciplinary expertise have a stake in the literacy development of youth (Vacca, 1998).

If secondary teachers want good students then they must do what they can to help their students become good readers. This is especially true for striving readers. Helping them become effective learners in content classrooms takes more than the efforts of the reading teacher or literacy coach alone. Every adult with whom striving readers interact during the school day shares responsibility for building positive relationships with them, heightening their engagement for learning, expanding their content knowledge, and leavening their literacy skills.

If administrators want teachers who employ responsive literacy practices then they must be leaders of initiatives to expand the literate culture of the school. Individual teacher efforts to increase students' reading and writing competency and efficacy are given more energy when they occur within the context of an overall schoolwide program with literacy development as a priority.

Principle 3: Responsive Literacy Instruction Provides Special Supports but not Always Special Settings

Fisher (2001) and others (Jacobson, Thrope, Fisher, Lapp, Frey, & Flood, 2001; Mastropieri et al., 2001) have demonstrated that striving readers are not always best served in pull-out programs and special classes. As we'll see in the next chapter, some approaches to RTI for reading at the secondary level attempt to keep students in the general education classroom as long as possible and return them there quickly if they are pulled out. However, RTI typically involves removing students from the classroom context at Tier 2 and certainly at Tier 3 (Vaughn & Klingner, 2007).

Cross-age tutoring, reading buddies, and a host of instructional modifications within the content classroom itself may do more to increase engagement and achievement. This may obviate the need for sequestering youth in homogenous groups of low-ability readers or isolating them for intensive skill work, which often occurs in schools where RTI is practiced.

Cappella and Weinstein (2001) found that most students who enter the 9th grade with reading problems leave high school with reading problems, suggesting the literacy issues striving readers bring to secondary schools are not receiving the attention they deserve. Classroom teachers who respond to the literacy needs of their striving readers will ensure they remain a part of the flow of instruction and enjoy the benefits of engaging learning experiences, regular print encounters, and instruction to build disciplinary knowledge.

Principle 4: Responsive Literacy Instruction Includes More Than a Curriculum of Basic Skills Redux

Striving readers are often penalized. They are usually recycled through a regimen of basic skill instruction that failed to produce reading competence in the first place (Allington, 2008). Basic skills instruction that focuses exclusively on phonics, spelling accuracy

and word attack, and requires memorization of rules and performing mechanical routines fails to capitalize on how language
is learned best (Ivey & Baker, 2004). Furthermore, skill instruction
in an area such as phonics has been shown to be most effective for
very young children with diminishing results for students in subsequent grades (National Reading Panel, 2000). When instruction
in these skills is embedded in meaningful content area reading and
learning, youth benefit by improving their ability to construct new
understandings (NCTE, 2004).

At the same time, I recognize that some adolescents bring re-
markably low reading achievement levels to secondary schools.
This leaves teachers and administrators grabbing for straws to
figure out how to elevate ability to help these students survive
in content classrooms but also pass mandated standardized tests.
Unlike RTI approaches for adolescents based on primary-grade
practices, it should not be assumed, however, that striving readers
require inordinate structure and routines to expand their language
and literacy abilities (Greenleaf, Schoenbach, Cziko, & Mueller,
2001; Ivey, 1999a; 1999b; Wassell, Hawrylak, & LaVan, 2010). Using reading and writing to help them explore personal interests
and satisfy cultural needs can increase their language competence
and their engagement in learning (Greenleaf, Jimenez, & Roller,
2002).

I learned of the power of supporting striving readers through
approaches that stress personally meaningful learning from a pro-
prietor of a local magic shop. Dean told me he was diagnosed as
learning disabled in the 2nd grade due to his inability to read. Dean
recounted how special education and reading teachers bombarded
him with daily skills sheets, phonics flash cards, and controlled
vocabulary booklets. After several years he experienced very little
reading improvement. Just when those teachers were ready to give
up on him, his 7th-grade math teacher discovered that Dean was
really interested in magic. The teacher gave him books on magic,
which Dean struggled through initially but eventually began reading with growing confidence. Soon he was able to apply his increasing reading skills to his school textbooks. Dean went on to graduate
from high school and, finally, from the University of Illinois with a
degree in business. He opened up his own magic store, which had
been operating profitably for several years when I met him.

Principle 5: Responsive Literacy Instruction Comes from Effective Teachers Who Have the Knowledge and Practices to Address Struggling Adolescent Readers' Needs

Students who feel their learning needs are not being met may exhibit a variety of bluffing and off-task behaviors (Brozo, 1990). I found many high school striving readers had learned how to "hide out" in disciplinary classrooms in order to avoid exposing their lack of reading competence. Some of the more common of these behaviors included

1. frequently forgetting to bring required books and other texts to class;
2. feigning attention by looking at teacher and nodding head but engaging in "mock participation" (Bloome & Green, 1984);
3. flagging hand and gestures to be called on when knows teacher calls on students thought not to be paying attention;
4. frequently putting head on the desk pretending to be tired or ill;
5. "apple polishing" and giving the teacher the impression of being cooperative and concerned; and
6. sitting next to a "with it" student for answers, directions, and help.

Many teachers are unable to recognize the lengths some striving students might go to keep from laying themselves bare before their peers or engaging in an activity that is painful and unrewarding. At the same time, some teachers have come to tolerate disengagement as long as it isn't disruptive by allowing striving readers to keep their heads on the desk or sit quietly by themselves. In any case, teachers are unwittingly exacerbating the problem of students hiding out if they lack practices for addressing it.

Secondary teachers who employ responsive literacy practices have a greater chance of bringing struggling learners out of hiding. These teachers understand that language and communication skills are equally important to teach as the substance of their disciplines. They know the importance of engagement and identity for adolescent learners. They also embrace their responsibility for the literacy development of all their students, not just the ones who "get it." When a high school biology teacher working with me in a school-wide literacy project discovered he had a stunning 15-grade-level spread in one of his classes, he put it this way, "Do you see why I teach to the middle?" He went on to explain that while he had empathy for the very low-ability readers, he did not feel competent enough to deal with their issues, and wondered why, as do many teachers in his situation, students with dismal reading skills are allowed to enter and progress through high school in the first place (Brozo & Hargis, 2003).

As an experienced university professor in teacher preparation and education programs, I know firsthand the extremely limited training secondary disciplinary teachers receive in practices for youth who are striving readers. So I acknowledge that higher education shares the blame in failing to meet the needs of teachers who must work with these students. But while reforms are desperately needed in teacher training programs, the issues striving adolescent readers bring to the classroom continue to mount.

School leaders need to do all they can to bolster teachers' competencies for addressing the literacy and learning needs of their striving students. And secondary teachers themselves need to accept personal responsibility for expanding their knowledge and abilities related not only to disciplinary literacy but also differentiated instruction. If anyone regards this latter admonishment as unrealistic, consider what Dong (2002) found in his study of high school biology teachers, who, when they focused on the academic welfare of striving English learners, developed creative practices that integrated language and content. In the end, RTI-like approaches at the secondary level will never achieve the level of success imagined by their proponents if teachers are not highly prepared and dispositionally given to responsive literacy instruction for all.

ACHIEVING A COMPREHENSIVE AND RESPONSIVE LITERACY PROGRAM AT THE SECONDARY LEVEL

As I argued in the opening to this chapter and reinforced with the principles above, when RTI is reframed as responsive literacy instruction, a comprehensive program of complimentary literacy practices can be achieved in secondary school contexts. A reframing of RTI is needed for two reasons already raised in this book. First, it is understood that RTI must be regarded as one of many possible approaches to meeting the federal government's support of measures schools take to prevent student literacy difficulties from developing and to address any existing difficulties students are experiencing. Second, there is little evidence that elementary-level RTI-like approaches can work in middle and high schools (Goetze, Laster, & Ehren, 2010), given the scarcity of practical cases and the complexities of those contexts.

In this section I demonstrate responsive and feasible ways of 1. determining the literacy abilities of all adolescent students; 2. expanding students' literacy capacities at all levels; and 3. acquiring regular feedback on students' understanding and growth as readers and learners. The approach I describe for a comprehensive and responsive secondary literacy program recasts the heretofore assumed features of RTI, such as universal screening, tiered interventions, and progress monitoring, in ways that are achievable within complex secondary school environments.

Determining the Literacy Abilities of All Students

Any comprehensive approach to literacy development for all must include methods of determining each student's abilities. In the parlance of RTI, this is referred to as *universal screening*. Universal screening fits the logic of RTI as appropriately tiered interventions cannot be initiated until it is known which tier would best serve a student (Fuchs & Fuchs, 2007).

Some secondary schools employing RTI-like practices use convenience data, such as high-stakes state test results, for universal screening. Although the availability of these whole-school assessments make them an attractive option for establishing each student's initial reading level, they have limitations. Most serious among them is that decisions made in August or September at the beginning of a new school year should be based on assessments made at that time and not on those from the previous spring, when state testing most often occurs. During the summer some adolescents might catch the reading bug or have positive experiences in a special reading program, elevating their skills and abilities beyond where they were the previous year. Conversely, some students will fall prey to the very real summer slide (Allington et al., 2010), and slip below their standing on spring testing.

In spite of their limitations, these spring testing data offer administrators and teachers opportunities to build consensus around students' literacy needs. For instance, I know middle and high school principals who use these assessments to demonstrate to their faculty the close relationship between reading achievement and student grades. When classroom teachers from every discipline see firsthand that students who perform below the 50th percentile in reading on the state test have the C's, D's, and F's, while students above the 50th percentile have A's and B's, they come to recognize that as they improve students' reading abilities they will likely have higher achievement from those students in their classrooms. It also makes it easier for school leaders to build a case for a total effort to improve teaching practices. When spring reading assessment data are used in this way, teachers and teacher leaders may be catalyzed to design and implement comprehensive literacy reforms.

An option to relying on extant student test data that may be as much as 3, 4, or 5 months old is to conduct schoolwide reading assessment at the outset of a new school year. The principal advantage of using this form of assessment is that information is obtained on reading achievement at the time when decisions are being made about whether special supports may be needed for students. On the negative side is the expense of purchasing commercially prepared standardized tests as well as the time and logistics involved in coordinating a schoolwide testing effort. Limitations aside, timely screening measures for possible reading challenges is the preferred option over using older extant test data.

I experienced firsthand the advantages of gathering timely reading achievement data in a yearlong high school literacy reform project in which I took part (Brozo & Hargis, 2003). Instead of relying on information from the state assessment from the previous spring, the school leaders purchased and authorized that standardized reading tests be administered to the entire student body in August to establish a baseline of need and again in May to determine if growth occurred after a program of initiatives were carried out. The low-stakes pre-post assessments—in this case the Nelson Denny Reading Test (NDRT) and Gates McGinitie Reading Test (GMRT), two highly-used and mature reading tests—were indexed to each student's reading level based on available data from the STAR test, a screening measure associated with the popular Accelerated Reader program (Renaissance Learning, http://www.renlearn.com/ar/).

Using this approach, we were able to assign the reading test that would match each student's actual reading level (as opposed to grade level), and be most sensitive to reading gains.

Some of the most enthusiastic RTI advocates (c.f., Fuchs & Fuchs, 2007) argue that Curriculum-Based Measurement (CBM) is the best option for screening as well as all other forms of assessment within an RTI approach. Ideally, CBM is comprised of a set of assessment methods created around the actual curricular materials and activities teachers are already using. For the primary grades this might include two or three dozen reading passages of equal difficulty, say all at the 2nd-grade level, with comprehension prompts. Initial screening might involve fluency and recall tasks with just one or two passages. Results might suggest particular areas of need (e.g., very slow reading, limited word recognition/ attack skills, weak comprehension). After the screening phase, the other parallel passages would be used throughout the year to determine the effectiveness of interventions.

At the secondary level, using CBM as a screening tool, although desirable, immediately takes on more complexity. As I have discussed in detail in Chapter 2 and pointed out in other places in this book, responsive instruction at the primary level focused on basic reading skills may be amenable to more pristine RTI practices, as recommended by its proponents; however, these same practices may not be as feasible with secondary-level readers. And with few if any examples to consult, it is difficult to say whether CBM can serve as a viable approach to reading screening in middle and high school.

If CBM for reading screening were to be carried out say, in a typical 10th-grade history class, it might take the form of passages taken from the primary course text and alternative text, such as those presented in electronic or hyperlinked formats. The traditional print passages would be short in length, perhaps no more than a page, accompanied by comprehension questions that tap various levels of thinking (i.e., literal, interpretive, applied, and critical) as well as knowledge of key concepts and vocabulary. They might also include prompts intended to gather written summaries or short responses to the text. The electronic reading assessment could be structured in a manner similar to online reading workshops recommended by Leu (2002):

- The teacher locates a site on the Internet with content related to a classroom unit of instruction and sets a bookmark for the location.
- The teacher designs an activity, inviting students to use the site as they accomplish content, critical literacy, or strategic knowledge goals in the curriculum.
- Students complete the research activity individually and independently, and then submit their work electronically.

The results of an assessment of this nature would alert the content classroom teacher to many potential reading and writing concerns with individual students who may require special literacy supports. Since the tasks are curriculum-embedded, they would reappear many times throughout the school year, allowing teachers and students to document the progress of reading and writing with traditional and electronic disciplinary text.

Another viable approach to screening students for possible literacy concerns in a secondary school classroom is the content-area reading inventory (Rakes & Smith, 1992). Like the other curriculum-embedded approaches to screening, this type of assessment is more informative than commercially prepared tests, since it provides insight into students' reading abilities with material from which they will need to learn throughout the year. The results of content-area inventory will show teachers which students are likely to have difficulty reading and thinking about assigned materials used in their course (Brozo & Simpson, 2007).

A typical content area reading inventory has two main sections (see Figure 3.1). The first one measures students' skills using book parts, reference features, and graphic material. Questions related to this part of the assessment are answered with the book or other reading source as a reference. The other part of the inventory is answered without access to the texts and involves answering comprehension and vocabulary questions for a text excerpt. Below are sample items that could be included in a content-area reading inventory for a high school math text.

It may be that there is no one ideal way of screening all students for possible literacy concerns in a typical middle or high school. Extant though older test data may be convenient and eliminate the

Figure 3.1. Content-Area Reading Inventory

Section I

Where would you find information about trigonometric functions?

Can the student use the table of contents effectively?

On what page can you find information on transition curves?

Is the student familiar with using an index?

On p. 109, what is the relationship between the drawing of the electrical wires in Example 3 and the graph below it?

Can the student understand the graphs used in the text?

If you were given a list of math vocabulary words and I wanted you to find their definitions, where would you check first?

Is the student familiar with glossaries?

Section II

What is a characteristic?

Tests explicit vocabulary knowledge.

What is a mantissa?

Tests explicit vocabulary knowledge.

Explain the meaning of the word *essential* as it is used in the following sentence: "An essential variable in the formula is the number of times a year the interest is compounded."

Tests implicit vocabulary knowledge. The student must use context clues or prior knowledge to define the term.

Where do exponential equations have applications?
(List one or more.)

This information is directly stated in the text.

The letter e represents a special number in mathematics. What type of logarithm uses e?

This information is directly stated in the text.

Why would a bank advertise that it compounds interest on savings continuously instead of compounding once each month?

The student must use reasoning skills to answer this question. The answer is not stated directly in the text.

need for individual teacher effort in the screening process, but not be as relevant or accurate. Employing screening techniques with actual disciplinary reading and writing secondary students must do may be immediately informative to classroom teachers, but will require significant involvement on their part to construct curriculum-embedded measures that screen for reading challenges. In the end, given the complexities and exigencies secondary schools, teachers, administrators, and students must balance issues of expense, time, and relevance if meaningful literacy screening is to occur.

Acquiring Regular Feedback on Students' Reading and Learning

Since the content classroom is the most important context for preventing and addressing reading and learning difficulties for students, it is within this environment regular checks of student growth should be obtained. However, if something like meaningful universal screening presents significant logistical and resource hurdles for secondary teachers and administrators, implementing ongoing systematic methods of monitoring student growth may be equally daunting. The process of acquiring formative feedback in secondary content classrooms presents at least a twofold challenge. One is finding the time for frequent consistent assessments; the other is crafting assessments that actually measure the literacy abilities needed for successful achievement in a particular discipline.

Remember, what students do in middle and high school is travel from classroom to classroom where they encounter a variety of teachers and disciplinary content throughout the day. The literacy demands of these content areas require much more than an overall ability to decode words and read with expression. The vocabulary, topics, and structure of disciplinary text necessitates a high degree of domain-specific knowledge, understanding of specialized word meanings, and the ability to organize thinking according to the linguistic patterns employed by authors. Consequently, anything like progress monitoring for literacy and learning in content classrooms must entail disciplinary-specific reading measures (Troia, 2006).

Thus, acquiring regular feedback on student reading and learning progress in the content classroom will necessitate measures of disciplinary literacy. These measures need to account for students' languaging and communication skills, such as the ability to understand disciplinary text, talk and write about topics from the disciplines, and present disciplinary information in various forms (National Council of Teachers of Mathematics, 2000). And these measures need to be embedded in the curriculum so they become part of the flow of instruction. In this way, secondary teachers of science, social studies, math, and the other subjects will be more likely to use the assessment process for documenting student growth.

The following curriculum-embedded assessment approaches have been shown to provide useful information about students' knowledge and literacy in secondary content classrooms.

Cloze/maze passages. Cloze/maze tasks require students to read a passage in which every nth word or a particular type of words has been deleted. When students come to the deletion, they must select the correct word from multiple options. Cloze/maze has been well-documented in the research literature as a viable approach to reading assessment (DuBay, 2004; Madelaine & Wheldall, 2004).

One important advantage of cloze/maze is classroom teachers can transform their every day text sources into short, informative assessments. Whether an excerpt from the course textbook, an information book, magazine, or some other material, when formatted as a cloze/maze task, students must demonstrate contextual reading skills as well as understanding of key domain-specific terminology.

Figure 3.2 provides an example from a science textbook demonstrating one possible format for structuring a cloze/maze passage. Teachers who use this approach can scan selected pages of text, convert to word document, then add highlighting and underlining to important terminology along with other words as foils. The cloze/maze passage can be projected on a SMARTboard or screen so an entire class can complete it at the same time. In this way, a disciplinary teacher can generate and administer content-specific formative assessments regularly and frequently. Individual charts can be maintained for and by each student to plot progress and monitor growth.

Vocabulary self-assessment. Students must have sufficient vocabulary knowledge if they are to comprehend disciplinary text (Marzano, 2005; Nagy & Scott, 2000). And yet, in many core academic subject area classrooms, instructional time for developing vocabulary knowledge has been found to be far from adequate (Flanigan & Greenwood, 2007; Scott, Jamieson-Noel, & Asselin, 2003).

Figure 3.2. Example of a Cloze/Maze Passage from Science

Suppose you could send a robot to another planet. What kinds of **1. *conduct, trials, experiments*** would you **2. *list, program, code*** the robot to carry out? Before you programmed the robot, you would need to figure out what **3. *information, order, rank*** you wanted it to **4. *arrange, gather, group***. Scientists are currently **5. *emerging, mounting, developing*** robots that they plan to send to Mars. These robots are being **6. *designed, deliberate, planned*** to examine the **7. *atmosphere, ambiance, population***, rocks, gravity, and magnetic **8. *meadows, fields, turfs*** of the planet.

Cloze/maze passages can be scored using the following criteria:

Percent of Correct Responses	Level
70–100	Independent
35–69	Instructional
0–34	Frustration

The following are useful ways of thinking about the three reading levels:

Independent. The level at which a reader can make maximum progress *without* teacher assistance. Students should be able to read texts at this level on their own for information and enjoyment. Text at this level is ideal for recreational, free-reading time.

Instructional. The level at which a reader can make maximum progress *with* teacher assistance. Varying degrees of teacher interaction and support should make instructional-level texts understandable for students. Otherwise, students will have difficulty comprehending text at this level if assigned as independent reading.

Frustration. The level at which a reader will not make progress *even with* teacher assistance. Frustration-level text is too difficult for students regardless of the level of instructional support provided by the teacher. It goes without saying, then, that teachers should do all they can to avoid assigning or using texts that are at the frustration level of their students.

There is a very close relationship between vocabulary knowledge and overall reading comprehension (Pearson, Hiebert, & Kamil, 2007; RAND Reading Study Group, 2002), but that relationship is even closer for content texts due to the numerous technical words and special word meanings (Harmon, Hedrick, & Wood, 2005).

Because students bring a range of word understandings to the learning of new topics in the content areas, it is important to assess students' vocabulary knowledge before reading or other tasks involving text (Fisher, Brozo, Frey, & Ivey, 2011). This awareness is valuable for students because it highlights their understanding of what they know, as well as what they still need to learn in order to fully comprehend the reading (Goodman, 2001).

Disciplinary teachers can provide students a list of important words at the beginning of the reading or unit and have students write them in a vocabulary self-assessment chart (see Figure 3.3). Students are asked to complete the chart before the lesson begins by rating each vocabulary word according to their level of familiarity and understanding. A plus sign (+) indicates a high degree of comfort and knowledge, a check mark (✓) indicates uncertainty, and a minus sign (–) indicates the word is brand new to them. Students should be encouraged to try to supply a definition and example for each word. For words with check marks or minus signs, students may have to make guesses about definitions and examples.

Figure 3.3. Example of a Vocabulary Self-Awareness Chart in American History

Word	+	✓	–	Example	Definition
segregation					
civil rights					
protest					
boycott					

Over the course of the reading or unit, content-area teachers should give students time to revisit their self-awareness charts to add new information and update their growing knowledge about key vocabulary. The goal is to bring all students to a comfortable level with the unit's important content terminology. Students should continually revisit their vocabulary charts to revise their entries. This also provides them with multiple opportunities to practice and extend their growing understanding of the words.

Since the process requires students to reflect on and document over time what they know about critical content-related terminology, vocabulary self-assessment is an ideal metacognitive tool. Moreover, because students have a record of their thinking about key concepts at different points in time, teachers have a ready-made indicator of progress.

Vocabulary matching. Another content literacy progress check that's relatively easy for secondary teachers to format and evaluate is a vocabulary matching task. Like the other formative assessments described in this section, vocabulary matching is premised on the particularly close relationship between word knowledge and reading comprehension of disciplinary text. Promising findings using this approach to predict content-area reading proficiency (Espin, Busch, Shin, & Kruschwitz, 2001; Espin & Foegen, 1996) suggest vocabulary matching can serve as a viable progress-monitoring tool in disciplinary classrooms.

In Figure 3.4, notice how simple it is to construct this curriculum-embedded assessment tool. Key vocabulary and concepts from disciplinary texts are listed with definitions. The students' task is to match the correct definition with the term. This task can be projected on a screen or SMARTboard, thus limiting the preparation time. A caveat, however; when considering whether to use this approach, a teacher must balance the ease of construction and administration with the fact that a matching task is not a particularly engaging one for students. And since engagement is a key factor in achievement, other approaches to formative assessment and progress monitoring, like those already described, may be more appropriate.

When using vocabulary matching, disciplinary teachers probe students' performance on a weekly or biweekly basis and graph the results. A graph presents a picture of performance that should be inspected by both the student and teacher to determine whether

Figure 3.4. Example of Vocabulary Matching Task in Science

1. Adaptation	a. community of organisms and its environment functioning as an ecological unit
2. Biome	b. organisms better adapted for survival will have more offspring increasing the chances that the traits of survival will increase
3. Climate	c. modification of an organism that makes it better able to live in its environment
4. Ecosystem	d. all the plants or animals of the same kind found in a given area
5. Environment	e. the average weather conditions over a period of years
6. Natural selection	f. a group of similar organisms capable of exchanging genes and interbreeding
7. Population	g. factors that act upon an organism that determine its form of survival
8. Species	h. a major ecological community (e.g., rainforest, desert

there is evidence of growth. If performance is not improving, the teacher and student should discuss possible reasons why and how instruction might change to be more responsive. Unlike grades and high-stakes tests, this procedure, like all the other curriculum-embedded approaches described in this section, is designed to promote responsive instruction in disciplinary classrooms that help prevent initial student failure.

Bubble maps. This approach to curriculum-embedded assessment is an alternative to vocabulary matching tasks for monitoring students' understanding of key disciplinary concepts. The visual structure and prompts of a bubble map may offer students a more interesting and potentially more engaging format. This approach, which goes by various names, such as semantic maps or concept ladders, uses a diagram in which students must identify and organize the relevant terms and concepts of a particular topic (see Figure 3.5).

Disciplinary teachers create a partially completed graphic that depicts networks of related terms and concepts, some of which are missing. Using a random list of the missing vocabulary, students are to supply the appropriate terms in their correct places on the bubble map. The advantage of the bubble map approach to simple matching approaches is that they provide insight into a student's ability to see connections and make critical links within a topic.

In conclusion, secondary disciplinary teachers have a variety of curriculum-embedded tools at their disposal for assessing student learning. These measures are relatively easy to format, administer, and make it possible for both students and teachers to reflect on progress and the effects of responsive content literacy instruction.

EXPANDING STUDENTS' LITERACY CAPACITIES AT ALL LEVELS WITH RESPONSIVE INSTRUCTION

Monitoring secondary students' disciplinary knowledge and literacy skills in middle and high school classrooms only makes sense within the context of an overall literacy program. As I have stated throughout this book, RTI is not so much a program with a long history of highly researched and established features as it is a response to IDEA for preventing and addressing reading and learning difficulties. In fact, there are no legal requirements in IDEA for RTI or any particular approach. Zirkel (2006) notes that:

Figure 3.5. Example of Bubble Map in Science

1. mass
2. temperature
3. heavenly motions
4. Kepler's 3rd Law

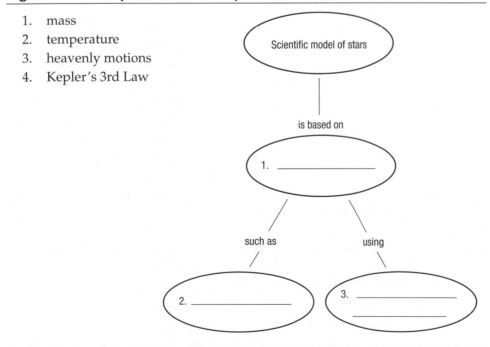

Scientific model of stars

is based on

1. _____

such as   using

2. _____   3. _____

There are many RTI models and the regulations are written to accommodate the many different models that are currently in use.
Thus, the USDE declined to endorse or elaborate any particular
model. (p. 2)

Furthermore, as has already been established, because most
RTI proponents come from a learning disabilities tradition, the approach tilts toward a remedial response to students' reading and
learning needs. It is also important to remind ourselves that many
variations and alternative approaches to RTI are possible and are
being tried in at least a few middle and high schools around the
United States (Deshler, Deshler, & Biancarosa, 2007; Gelzheiser,
Scanlon, & Hallgren-Flynn, 2010).

Establishing a comprehensive program that supports literacy
development for secondary students at all levels requires a vision
of responsive instruction that places emphasis on 1. creating a rich
and vibrant overall literate culture in the school, 2. prevention over
intervention 3. creative services for meeting the needs of students
with serious reading difficulties, and 4. building engaged literate
identities for adolescents.

Creating a Rich Literate School Culture

In a very real sense, the true Tier 1 of RTI, or for that matter
any comprehensive literacy program, is the school culture. The
overall school culture is comprised of many facets that either nur-
ture, ignore, or stifle the development of youths' positive literacy
attitudes, practices, and identities (Hinchman, Alvermann, Boyd,
Brozo, & Vacca, 2003/2004; Sturtevant, Boyd, Brozo, Hinchman,
Alvermann, & Moore, 2006). To reach adolescent youth as readers,
bolster their literate identities, and sustain their efforts as readers and learners requires an entire school effort (Brozo & Hargis,
2003). To this end, overall school leadership and literacy leadership are paramount.

Leadership. Secondary school leaders have enormous influence
on the direction and implementation of literacy initiatives (Deshler,
Deshler, & Biancarosa, 2007). Supovitz and Weinbaum (2008), in assessing a variety of high school literacy reform efforts, argue for the
centrality of school leaders by asserting:

> Their advocacy plays a huge role in setting the context and estab-
> lishing the agenda for reform. Without the weight and legitimacy
> of their support, reforms often crumble from lack of priority and
> inattention. (p. 167)

Leaders who dedicate themselves to ensuring a schoolwide commitment to certain practices are more likely to see those practices enacted (Ogle & Hunter, 2001). Virtually all successful secondary literacy programs have district- and school-level leaders providing sustained support to teachers and students (Langer, 2002; 2004).

Literacy leaders may have the most influence on any comprehensive literacy program. With a proactive disposition and positive interactions with individuals and groups of teachers and administers, a literacy leader can help define a school's expectations for literacy teaching and learning (Coburn, 2001; Sturtevant, 2003). Together with school leaders, an engaged and committed literacy leader can do a great deal to elevate the literate culture of a secondary school in ways that visitors to the school might sense without realizing it. They might notice a busy library with numerous students checking out books, students walking down halls carrying paperbacks, and banners and marquees proclaiming literacy-related events, such as an author in-residence and a sustained silent reading schedule. A visitor might also overhear teachers in a work room sharing successes with literacy instruction and planning literacy lessons.

Sustained print encounters of student-selected texts. By establishing SSR—Sustained Silent Reading time or other similar opportunities (DEAR—Drop Everything and Read; DIRT—Daily Individual Reading Time), school and literacy leaders can make certain every student is engaged with text of their choosing on a regular basis. RTI approaches, with their emphasis on interventions, might go a long way toward preventing reading difficulties if they made room for daily uninterrupted reading. Creating time and space during the school day for recreational, self-selected reading allows students to read about their interests, discover new interests, gain skill and background knowledge, and develop a habit of reading (Krashen, 2004). An added benefit is that as students expand their word knowledge and overall abilities as readers, their school achievement tends to improve as well (Brozo & Simpson, 2007).

Most youth, by the time they reach middle and high school, have mastered basic reading skills. From there, the surest road to a richer vocabulary and expanded literacy is wide and sustained reading (Allington, 2002; Cipielewski & Stanovich, 1992; Taylor, Frye, & Maruyama, 1990). Some adolescents' reading difficulties can be traced to their lack of interest in and downright avoidance of print experiences (Beers, 1996; 2003). The more time students spend with books and print, the more growth they exhibit on measures of vocabulary and reading achievement (Gardiner, 2001; Krashen, 2004).

The key, according to Krashen (2004), is fidelity and perseverance when it comes to SSR and other such approaches. He has found that such programs of longer duration have a more durable impact on student achievement and attitudes. This is where the role of school leaders in sustaining teacher and staff commitment is vital.

In a high school literacy reform project I collaborated on with the reading coach, the SSR initiative named by students Reading Cyclone, was launched to ensure all students, regardless of ability, developed the reading habit, and all teachers participated in modeling the pleasure of self-selected reading. Using grant funds, the librarian and English department head purchased scores of high interest young adult novels and magazines covering a wide range of reading levels, which were compiled into class sets. Metal racks were pulled from a school district warehouse and placed in every teacher's classroom to hold the SSR material. Drop boxes were set up at several locations in the building, and students were encouraged to donate a favorite paperback to the cause. This netted many additional books that were added to the classroom libraries. One day per week during homeroom, approximately 25 minutes, was set aside for SSR; although many teachers added days on their own as they discovered the advantages of having students involved in focused, constructive activity and as they themselves discovered the enjoyment of recreational reading during the school day.

Advocates of literacy reform in secondary schools (Alvermann, Boyd, Brozo, Hinchman, Moore, & Sturtevant, 2002; Beers, Probst, & Reif, 2007; Deschler, Palincsar, Biancarosa, & Nair, 2007; Langer, 2002) concur that students need multiple opportunities for engaged, sustained print encounters in the classroom every day. Furthermore, the easier the access to interesting print materials, the more frequently adolescents read (McQuillan & Au, 2001). Lack of opportunities for regular, engaged reading may help account for why most students who are poor readers upon entry into high school remain at the low or basic reading level at the time of graduation (Cappella & Weinstein, 2001). We know, however, that when a whole school commits itself to providing students significant opportunities for wide reading, preventive measures within that same context have a greater likelihood of success (Fisher & Ivey, 2006).

Preventing Reading Failure

When an entire school makes a commitment to students' reading development and engagement with text through regular opportunities for self-selected, sustained print encounters, an important first step in the prevention of reading failure has already begun. Within an overall school context supportive of adolescent literacy, any other related initiatives will be reinforcing and are likely to bring about achievement gains (Brozo & Hargis, 2003).

It is important to remember that IDEA 2004 stipulates 15% of the monies used for learning disabilities programs should be devoted to prevention. This is no small matter, as countless school districts around the United States receive large sums of federal dollars for special education services. RTI advocates, as noted, boast that its system of universal screening, progress monitoring, and tiers of increasingly targeted interventions works against the "wait and fail" approach of many prevailing learning disabilities programs. It is critical to point out here that although IDEA is a set of regulations for individuals with disabilities in education, there is nothing in the Act barring teachers outside of special education from delivering RTI or any other literacy support service (Allington, 2008). Indeed, the National Association of State Directors of Special Education (NASDE, 2007) has made clear that:

> RTI is not something that happens in special education. Rather it is a method for teaching all students that needs to be driven by general education teachers. (p. 2)

If RTI or any conception of preventive and interventive instruction is a general education concern, because it's intended for all students, then the frontline of prevention of literacy difficulties in

(text continues on p. 80)

RTI in the Real World

CHEYENNE MOUNTAIN JUNIOR HIGH SCHOOL

Cheyenne Mountain Junior High School began implementation of the RTI process during the 2006 – 2007 school year. With an increasingly diverse population, educators recognized the need for a schoolwide intervention process aimed at improving instruction. The existing schoolwide behavioral support program that utilizes a problem-solving approach with a tiered model of service delivery was expanded to address academic concerns through the RTI process. The goal of expanding the program was to ensure that appropriate learning opportunities for all students were being provided, beginning in the general education classrooms.

At the time of implementing RTI there was no system for universal screening and therefore no system for providing early intervention for students with potential learning problems. Currently, the Diagnostic Assessment of Reading (DAR) is used to screen for reading. Students who score at or below the 5th-grade level are then targeted for Tier 2 intervention. The school also established a process to collect, review, and analyze student data using curriculum-based assessments in reading, writing, and mathematics. This critical stage allows the school's Problem-Solving Team (PST) to assign appropriate supports and interventions early on. The PST is also responsible for monitoring student progress and modifying the interventions based on individual progress. This ongoing process is critical to the success of the RTI process. It is through this process that teachers constantly collect and analyze evidence of student performance, which in turn is used to inform instructional decisions or to refer students to other levels of intervention.

Tier 1. At the Tier 1 level, students are provided evidence-based instruction, positive behavioral support, and other accommodations. In order to improve instruction in the general education classroom, teachers received professional development on ways to differentiate instruction in the classroom. This has resulted in an increased capacity for the application of strategies as well as an awareness of the different types of learners and the various ways in which their learning needs can be met in the general education classroom. In conjunction with differentiated instruction, unit pre-assessments are being used, which allow the teacher to determine the appropriate placement of students within a range of assignments and activities for a given lesson. Instruction is revised throughout the lesson based on formative assessments that inform the teacher on when and how to modify the lesson or student groups to ensure student comprehension.

Tier 2. Students who do not achieve grade level standards with the Tier 1 supports are referred to Tier 2. The Tier 2 level is a short-term intervention (8 to 12 weeks) aimed at helping students acquire specific academic skills through the use of small group instruction and regular progress monitoring. Students in the Tier 2 interventions also benefit from the supports that are given in the general education classrooms.

One of the accommodations for literacy support is the literacy lab elective. Students who are identified for intervention are asked to use one of their elective credits to enroll in the literacy lab elective. The lab is staffed with a reading specialist who utilizes the Language!™ program along with other supported reading activities to increase student reading success. Advance organizers are another accommodation provided for these students to support comprehension in their general education classrooms.

The after-school tutoring program has been one of the more effective interventions offered. Half of the students who are enrolled in this program have made significant gains in reading comprehension. Based on the success of the after-school tutoring program, plans are under way to create an "access" period at the end of the day that will allow students to access teachers or other students in order to receive needed help.

Tier 3. The early identification and interventions that are provided by utilizing the RTI process have limited the number of students requiring Tier 3 interventions. Students are identified for Tier 3 through progress monitoring. When students fail to make sufficient progress in the classrooms with the interventions provided by the Tier 1 and Tier 2 supports, they are recommended for Tier 3 interventions, which are tailored to the needs of each individual student.

CRITICAL QUESTIONS:

- What kind of curriculum-based assessments might be most useful to monitor progress of students' reading abilities at Cheyenne Mountain Junior High? Why?
- What could evidence-based instruction in Tier 1 look like? How can disciplinary teachers at Cheyenne Mountain Junior High provide responsive literacy instruction at Tier 1?
- Suggest ways students with reading challenges at Cheyenne Mountain Junior High could receive accommodations in the Tier 1 setting so they remain in the general education classroom.

middle and high school must be the content classroom. The implications of which are clear—a substantial level of responsibility for meeting the needs of all readers and learners rests with classroom teachers and the literacy specialists who support them.

In Chapter 2, I explored several potential problems with trying to impose an elementary-level version of RTI on a typical secondary-level school. Two of the principal differences are that unlike elementary schools, typical secondary schools are divided into disciplines and departments, and, perhaps because of this departmentalization, middle and high school teachers often see themselves first and foremost as content experts. Penetrating this culture with its rigid discipline dividers and teachers' perceptions of efficacy tied to their content knowledge is always a challenge, but a worthwhile one when the goal is to create an environment in which every teacher supports the literacy development of all students.

Prevention at the whole-class level. Secondary content classroom teachers could go a long way toward building and reinforcing literacy skill while limiting potential reading difficulties by incorporating disciplinary literacy practices into their daily instruction. In addition to useful generalizable strategies for processing any text that students can learn (Brozo & Simpson, 2007), it is becoming increasingly clear that texts in each subject area, whether math, science, or history, present unique reading demands on students and require specialized strategies (Shanahan & Shanahan, 2008).

There are literally hundreds of content literacy strategies available to secondary classroom teachers. Because there are so many it can become a daunting task just trying to determine which ones may have the most significant impact on student learning. This is where the reading specialist or literacy coach can be especially helpful. In my own professional development projects for secondary teachers, I like to present a range of possible strategies for each phase of a good lesson (see Table 3.1, showing sample strategies at the three lesson phases), and then make sure teachers have the opportunity to experiment with the strategies to gain firsthand experience. It's essential that content teachers are provided guided scaffolding by a professional developer or literacy specialist as they take their first steps toward strategy implementation. This can take the form of demonstration teaching, joint lesson planning, team teaching, or observations with debriefing.

Table 3.1. Sample Content Literacy Strategies for Different Phases of Lesson

Readiness	Interactive Comprehension	Extending New Learning
SQPR	Questioning the Author	RAFT writing
Anticipation Guide/ Opinionnaire	Reciprocal Teaching	SPAWN writing
Text Impression	GISTing	Story Chains
Vocabulary Self-Awareness	Split-Page Notetaking	Vocabulary cards

To demonstrate how whole-class methods can be employed to encourage maximum participation in text processing, let's consider an example of how a Readiness Phase content literacy strategy might be conducted. Ms. Vasquez introduces her 7th-grade social studies students to the chapter in their history texts on the Bill of Rights in the U.S. Constitution with a Student Questions for Purposeful Reading (SQPR) activity. SQPR begins with the teacher presenting the class with a thought-provoking statement related to the content students are about to read and study. In pairs or small groups students then generate questions they would like answered based on the statement.

Ms. Vasquez projects the following statement on the board:

The U.S. Constitution guarantees the right for you to go anywhere you like on the Internet.

She asks students to find a partner and brainstorm one or two questions they want answered. Ms. Vasquez walks around the room to provide any needed assistance and clarify the task. She also sits in with a few pairs and offers her own important questions to make certain they are asked. After a few minutes she invites students to share their questions, and as they do Ms. Vasquez writes them on the board, putting stars next to those asked more than once by other multiple pairs. Some samples include:

1. Where in the Bill of Rights does it say this?
2. What other rights do I have that are protected in the Constitution?

3. Does the Constitution give me the right to swear anytime I want?
4. Does the Bill of Rights protect me because I'm a Muslim?
5. What rights are in the Constitution for kids my age?
6. How are the Constitution and Bill of Rights different?

Once all pairs share their questions, Ms. Vasquez draws attention to the ones with multiple stars and urges the class to make sure that among all the questions on the board, the class consensus questions get answered. At this point, Ms. Vasquez has her students engage with the lesson text, which is a primary document accessed online that includes the actual Bill of Rights along with expert analysis written at a level appropriate for middle grades students. Students read excerpts from relevant sections of this text, while also listening to explanations and examples from Ms. Vasquez.

At regular intervals, students work with their partners to find answers to the priority and other questions they generated in the SQPR activity. Also during this time, Ms. Vasquez asks the class which questions could be answered based on the text covered to that point. She makes time for answers to be discussed, elaborated, confirmed, or revised. When satisfied with an answer, students write the question and answer individually into their learning logs.

Teachers like Ms. Vasquez who routinely and reflexively imbed literacy strategy instruction into their daily lessons, will improve the chances of keeping all students engaged and learning. In this way, her practices of braiding text content with literacy strategies should help limit those students who might otherwise struggle to read and keep up. Nonetheless, in spite of her best efforts, there will be some students who will continue to find it difficult to profit from the required readings and class activities without extra support. For these students, instruction that responds to their greater reading and learning needs could first be delivered within the classroom context. The next section describes what this form of instruction might look like.

Within-class differentiated instruction. At the point when any student needs extra support, whether indicated on broad level or formative assessments, in RTI parlance some form of intervention is required. Another way to put it, of course, is to say more responsive instruction is warranted. For reasons argued in previous chapters,

I prefer a responsive instruction over interventionist perspective, since it is less clinical and deficit-driven. Furthermore, the notion of responsive instruction assumes there is no one superior way to reach and teach disengaged and striving readers. Regardless of the terminology one prefers, deciding best practices for struggling readers is the essential challenge.

I agree with Fisher and Ivey (2006) who reinforce a point made earlier in this chapter by asserting "Without . . . access to high-quality, readable texts and instruction in strategies to read and write across the school day—it is doubtful that a specific, limited intervention will make much of a difference" (p. 181). Thus, any special literacy support must be offered within a broader supportive context for adolescents' literacy development. Fisher and Ivey (2006) go on to propose four essential criteria for making fundamental changes in the literate lives of striving youth: 1. The teacher should play a critical role in assessment and instruction; 2. the intervention should reflect a comprehensive approach to reading and writing; 3. reading and writing in the intervention should be engaging; and 4. the intervention should be driven by useful and relevant assessments.

Let's return to Ms. Vasquez's 7th-grade social studies class for insights into how a quality teacher might respond within the classroom to a student's need for additional literacy supports.

One of her students, Marfa, came to the middle school nearly a month after the start of the academic year. While Marfa's academic file from her previous school had yet to arrive, Ms. Vasquez wasted no time in conducting an assessment of her reading abilities with an informal inventory (Brozo & Afflerbach, 2011). To gauge Marfa's knowledge and skills in middle school history, Ms. Vasquez has her read passages taken directly from social studies textbooks and accompanying booklets at the 6th-, 7th-, and 8th-grade levels. She documents patterns of miscues or decoding errors, takes note of the accuracy and quality of her answers to comprehension questions, and has her write summaries and outlines for each passage. Ms. Vasquez's overall analysis of Marfa's performance on the inventory is that she is capable at best of successful reading with 6th-grade texts, one year below the class level, and only with consistent instructional support.

After a couple of weeks of documenting Marfa's responses to and progress on near-daily curriculum-embedded assessments, such as vocabulary self-assessment and cloze/maze activities, it becomes clear to Ms. Vasquez that Marfa is struggling to keep up. Because time in a class with 25 students limits opportunities for one-to-one interaction, Ms. Vasquez realizes she needs to provide Marfa resources she can use on her own during daily lessons and independent work time.

One of the first instructional modifications Ms. Vasquez makes for Marfa is to provide her copies of articles on history topics being covered in class that are easier to read than the textbook and other typical sources. Using Internet sites such as Ben's Guide to U.S. Government for Kids (http://bensguide.gpo.gov/), Ms. Vasquez finds, reformats, and prints numerous passages on American history. She puts attractive covers on these readings and makes them available to Marfa and any other students who are finding it difficult to access content with the classroom text sources. Ms. Vasquez's rationale for using simpler topically-related texts is they: 1. provide needed print experiences for struggling readers like Marfa, and 2. help build important background knowledge in history.

Another modification Ms. Vasquez makes for students like Marfa is to provide process guides for reading required text. Readers who find it difficult to read and learn from material independently can be provided scaffolding in the form of directions, questions, and prompts to support their text processing. Again, because Ms. Vasquez does not have much time or many opportunities to work one-on-one with Marfa, the process guides she supplies her serve as the next best thing to an individualized tutorial.

As students progress through information sources, learning about a content area topic, their processing of the information and concepts can be guided. Process guides scaffold students' comprehension within unique formats. They're designed to stimulate students' thinking during or after their reading. Guides also help students focus on important information and ideas, making their reading more efficient (Kintsch, 2005; Kintsch & Kintsch, 2005). Process guides prompt thinking, ranging from simple recall to connecting information and ideas to prior experience, applying new knowledge, and problem solving (Best, Rowe, Ozuru, & McNamara, 2005).

Ms. Vasquez creates a process guide for Marfa by first reading the text material thoroughly in order to decide which information and concepts need to be emphasized and aspects of the text that might pose the biggest challenges to comprehension. She determines how much assistance Marfa will need to construct and use meaning. If Ms. Vasquez knows Marfa already possesses a basic understanding of content, she crafts a guide that emphasizes higher level thinking. On the other hand, if the content is new to Marfa, then she creates a guide that balances text-based and high-level processing.

As she develops the guide (see Figure 3.6), Ms. Vasquez considers a format that will stimulate Marfa to think about the text in meaningful ways. She also constructs the guide so that it will motivate and appeal to Marfa. When Marfa is given her first process guide, Ms. Vasquez explains its features, goals, and benefits. She demonstrates how to use the guide to focus on key terms and ideas in the text. She emphasizes the importance of Marfa being responsible for explaining her responses to the guide prompts.

Figure 3.6. Sample Process Guide Prompts for a Chapter in a History Textbook

1. In the section under Afghanistan you will learn the background of this country and why there is so much unrest there. Now read the first paragraph. **Be prepared to explain the term** *Taliban*.

The Taliban is _____

2. The paragraph on page 66 will discuss some events caused by the Taliban. Read the paragraph carefully. **List below some of the events connected with the Taliban:**

The Taliban did these things: _____
_____

3. On page 67 the last paragraph of this section tells us whether or not the Taliban has been successful in its attempt to control Afghanistan. Read the paragraph and decide. Write your response here:

Ms. Vasquez's practices that differentiate instruction within her 7th-grade history classroom are designed to ensure students like Marfa acquire needed disciplinary knowledge and literacy skill in the most supportive environment. The goal for Ms. Vasquez is to help as many of her students as possible remain in her classroom, and avoid pull-out services that may take them into learning settings without the same level of support she provides and where students may fail to gain vital content knowledge.

CREATIVE SERVICES FOR MEETING THE NEEDS OF STUDENTS WITH SERIOUS READING DIFFICULTIES

It's important to remind ourselves of two key points as we continue this discussion of responsive literacy practices for all students. The first is that IDEA 2004 does not specify or privilege any particular approach to addressing the learning needs of students. Thus, RTI stands as one approach among many. This is especially the case with RTI for literacy at the secondary level, where the research base is virtually nonexistent, and practical school-based examples are few and far between. The second point is there is nothing in IDEA that requires special educators be the service providers to striving readers and learners.

I reiterate these critical points to make clear that many viable options are open to secondary school teachers, school leaders, and literacy specialists for preventive and interventive services. Consequently, in the situation in which a middle or high school student exhibits serious difficulties reading and learning in the general education classroom, there are instructional possibilities that go beyond traditional learning disabilities/remedial approaches.

It is unfortunate that approaches to teaching remedial reading for older students have tended to emphasize learning discreet skills. For instance, some have recommended graphosyllabic analysis as one way to improve reading fluency and spelling (Archer, Gleason, & Vachon, 2003; Bhattacharya & Ehri, 2004). Others stress phonics and word study work as the most efficient way to address serious reading concerns adolescents bring to secondary classrooms (Blevins, 2001). Although adolescent striving readers may exhibit weaknesses in these areas based on diagnostic reading tests, instruction targeted to these skills as with skill instruction of any kind needs to be considered within the context of authentic literacy practices (Ivey & Baker, 2004), and taught in ways to develop independent reading abilities (Harmon, 2002). The problem with focusing reading instruction for older students on discreet skills is that they can demonstrate mastery on worksheets, only to fail to transfer that mastery to naturally occurring text while reading independently (Harmon, 2000). Consequently, skills training should only be provided striving adolescent readers if it translates into successful meaning making of real texts.

What often gets left out of the conversation about older striving readers when discussed from a learning disabilities perspective, is the issue of engagement (Guthrie, 2008) and self-efficacy (Alvermann, 2003). For adolescents who lack fundamental reading skills, it is paramount that they not be forced to participate in a program of remediation that fails to hold their interest or that they perceive as humiliating. If so, there is little chance they will persevere long enough for the program to be of any benefit to them as regards achievement or self-efficacy (Yudowitch, Henry, & Guthrie, 2008). Furthermore, we want our instruction to be high impact so as to become a part of a student's reading skill set for life. To be clear, I'm not questioning whether seriously striving readers need basic skills, but what I am questioning is how those readers will be apprenticed to acquire and develop needed skills.

One of the principles to guide responsive literacy instruction at the secondary level presented earlier in this chapter stipulates that striving readers should not be required to repeat a regimen of remedial instruction if it failed to improve achievement and capacity the first time. Similarly, RTI advocates urge the use of progress monitoring tools to determine whether interventions are having the desired effect. If not, the intervention should be modified. This is, in fact, responsive instruction, because teachers do not assume that the fault lies within the student if a particular practice or approach doesn't work. Instead, modifications to instruction continue to be made in an effort to find which one or combination bring about higher engagement and achievement.

The following are creative approaches to supporting the more serious reading needs of adolescents. Nonetheless, the effectiveness of these approaches like any form of responsive instruction relies on flexibility and close monitoring of students' attitudes and achievement.

Cross-Age Tutoring

Sixteen-year-old Brandon began the 10th grade resigned to the idea that he would be a dropout before year's end. His two older brothers had done so, and his sister was receiving homebound instruction after having a baby. Paula, the literacy coach working in Brandon's school, was launching a buddy reading program that year and recognized, after looking through Brandon's file, that he was an ideal candidate for the program. Her cross-age tutoring program was part of an overall plan to identify and target youth who needed extra reading-skill support, and who were at risk of leaving school. In spite of Brandon's lack of motivation and low reading scores, which were between the 6th- and 7th-grade levels, his teachers characterized him as cooperative, helpful, and friendly.

Paula had made arrangements with the elementary school to host tutorial sessions twice weekly, involving 2nd- and 3rd-graders and high school reading buddies. Fortunately, the elementary school was only a short walk across the track field from the high school.

Paula spoke about participating as a buddy reader to Brandon and several other students who had low reading achievement and were at-risk of dropping out. He agreed to give it a try, especially when he realized he would be able to leave his third-block study hall, which turned out to be an ideal time to conduct the tutoring. Paula prepared Brandon and five others for their roles as reading tutors. They were taught techniques for discovering children's interests and how to do a read aloud of a children's book. They learned how to facilitate writing in response to reading and how to make books. They also were taught strategies for teaching vocabulary and helping their younger buddies decode difficult words.

Throughout the training, Paula stressed to Brandon and the others that one of the primary goals of the tutoring program was not only to help their young reading buddies improve as readers but also to discover the joy of reading and writing. Above all, Paula hoped that Brandon and his adolescent partners would expand their own reading and writing skills as a result of developing literacy strategies for helping younger, less able readers than themselves.

Brandon was paired with a 3rd-grader named Gabe, who, according to his teacher and the reading coach, was exhibiting difficulties and frustration with reading grade-appropriate materials. The cross-age tutoring sessions took place in the elementary school's media center, where computers were available throughout the large open room. They spent the first tutorial session getting to know one another. Brandon was surprised to learn in their first meeting that Gabe lived in the same housing project only a couple of streets from Brandon's building. The two hit it off right away as they explored their mutual love of football. Gabe told Brandon his father lived in Chicago, and that was the team he wanted to play for when he grew up. Gabe also told Brandon that he wanted his own computer so he could play "cool games."

Before the session ended, Brandon read a few pages he had rehearsed from a short biography of Michael Jordan. Gabe enjoyed the book and asked if he would come back and read some more from it. Brandon reassured him he would return in a couple of days. Not all the tutors could give such assurances, as some of them started dropping out over the coming weeks and months. Brandon, however, stuck it out and enjoyed his newfound status as a role model and "expert" reader for Gabe.

The focus of most of their work together was football. Paula and the elementary school librarian assisted the pair by finding easy-to-read, high-interest books and texts on football related topics. The boys especially enjoyed reading together biographies of great Bears players from the past, such as Dick Butkus, Walter Payton, Jim McMahon, and the "Fridge" Perry. One activity Paula suggested was to keep an electronic scrapbook of the Bears that season. Brandon and Gabe used Digital Storytelling software made available to them by the librarian to write descriptions of their favorite players, insert images, video and voice clips, as well as tables and figures of statistics and trivia from player's records.

While finding images on the Internet of the Bears' premier middle linebacker, Brian Urlacher, also known as "The Beast," Gabe had much to say about his powerful physique, wondering out loud how it's possible to become so muscular. Brandon had become used to following up on Gabe's curiosities and interests in their cross-age tutoring sessions, so thought that information about football players fitness and body building regimens could be researched.

Using descriptors such as "football players training" and "NFL players fitness," they were able to locate sites that described how players worked out with weights and built muscle mass. Brandon was intrigued by references at one of the sites to performance enhancement drugs. He talked with Paula about the merits of pursuing this topic further with Gabe, and she thought it was a good idea. Paula helped Brandon find objective and easy-to-read information about fitness supplements and drugs in the high school library and on the Internet.

Although Paula liked the topic, she was concerned about how Brandon would share this content with Gabe. She worked with Brandon to make sure he wouldn't inadvertently glorify drug use for an impressionable boy in order to acquire a super-sized physique. Together, they developed strategies for sharing selected content from the resources they found that would help Gabe begin to appreciate the drug-free ways of building muscle and stamina for athletic competition.

Aware of Gabe's keen interest in computers, Brandon came up with the idea of digital activity related to the topic by examining and modifying characters from popular computer games. Brandon and Gabe had read in one of the short pieces they found on the Internet that playing games such as *True Crime: Streets of LA* (Activision) and *WWF Wrestlemania* (THQ) was a common pastime for American football players when on the road or during the off-season. Brandon asked Gabe whether he thought many football players and body builders envied and wanted to resemble the heroes and villains in these games who often have exaggerated muscles. Paula was impressed with Brandon's ability to reason critically by recognizing how these images might influence certain athletes to do whatever it takes, including using drugs, to achieve unusual physiques.

The elementary media specialist helped Brandon and Gabe use the Internet to find computer game figures from *Take No Prisoners* (Red Orb), *The Hulk* (Vivendi-Universal), *Army Men: Sarge's Heroes* (3DO), and *X-Men: Mutant Academy* (Activision). Then they downloaded the pictures into Adobe Photoshop to alter them. The reading buddies experimented with program to reshape the main character's physiques in ways that were more proportional to normal muscle development. Their work resulted in a brief Power-Point show with "before" slides, accompanied by captions warning of the dangers of steroids and other illegal substances for building muscle, and "after" slides with statements about good health, diet, and fitness. Paula allowed the proud pair to share the slides with others in the cross-age tutoring program, and the elementary school's principal was impressed enough to make sure the slides were shown to children during drug awareness events that year.

Paula's buddy reading program created the opportunity for striving readers like Brandon and Gabe to establish a positive relationship around reading and writing. This approach allowed Brandon as an adolescent reader a context for expanding his skills and motivation while enlarging his self-efficacy through positive role modeling. At the same time, it offered Gabe, a 3rd-grader in need of extra reading supports, an enjoyable and engaging way to have additional print experiences. Both boys demonstrated improvement in reading on the year-end state test. Brandon's overall school performance improved, as well, leading his decision to return to school as an 11th-grader.

In spite of its effectiveness for Brandon and Gabe, cross-age tutoring as a way of working with low-performing readers is not likely to become a common feature of RTI. And yet, it epitomizes the goal of responsive literacy instruction by its focus on the reader's needs and its flexible response options.

Community Partners as Reading Mentors

Paula's approach to improving Brandon's and other adolescent striving readers' abilities was to turn them into reading buddies to much younger striving readers. Another form of cross-age tutoring involves bringing together adolescent struggling readers and mentors from the community.

One such mentoring program was established by Katrina, whose second block freshmen English class was comprised of students who had low reading scores on the state achievement test. In the class, Katrina was employing a range of responsive literacy practices to build students' skill and will to read, but knew some additional print experiences in a supportive context would accelerate growth. The goal of the program was to use community volunteers to read to the most seriously struggling readers. Katrina challenged all her volunteers to be as resourceful as possible in creating motivating reading experiences, not by teaching reading, per se—which was what she was doing in the classroom—but by teaching the pleasures and benefits of reading.

Lionel hadn't given a thought to volunteering before he saw an advertisement about Katrina's program in the local paper. He had recently retired from a career as an Army intelligence officer and was casting about for something to keep him occupied while he considered his next career options. He loved to read and had exciting and varied life experiences to bring to the tutorial setting. Moreover, since boys comprised most of the school's lowest achieving readers, Lionel could be an ideal mentor to bring about improvement in attitude and achievement for a male youth in the program.

Katrina formed a partnership between Lionel and Marcus, a 14-year-old freshman with a reading level equivalent to grade 5. Marcus had an IEP (Individualized Education Plan) based on his learning disability in reading. The plan stipulated that Marcus could receive a variety of reading services, including one-on-one tutoring, so Katrina got approval from the special education director, Marcus's case worker, and Marcus's mother for him to work with a reading mentor.

Marcus's home situation had been especially challenging. The previous year, his mother moved the family into a motel room on a noisy highway. Marcus spent some of that year in an alternative school until his behavior warranted a transfer back to his local high school. After finding a better job and more permanent living quarters, Marcus's mother was working closely with the school to help him improve his reading skills.

In order to receive reading mentoring from Lionel, Marcus's learning disabilities teacher agreed to excuse him for 45 minutes during her first block self-contained English/reading class, which met 3 days per week. Lionel and Marcus met in a room adjacent to the library reserved for student clubs.

The first couple of sessions were taken up with conversation about each of their interests. Marcus wanted to know about Lionel's military experiences, and Lionel learned about the numerous family and academic challenges Marcus had already confronted as a young teen. They took Katrina up on her suggestion to put together "my bags" to share their interests. Lionel brought an army duffle bag with items to share, while Marcus put items in his backpack. Specifically, Lionel discovered that Marcus liked to draw, listen to music, have hands-on experiences, and snack while learning. This helped break the ice and gave Lionel ideas about how to motivate Marcus and which texts and literacy activities might appeal to him.

With Katrina's approval, Lionel used graphic novels as the primary source for working on reading with Marcus. He reasoned that because of Marcus's interest in drawing and his limited comprehension abilities, a graphic novel would be engaging and easier to comprehend with illustrations to accompany the text. Because Lionel didn't know how to teach reading in the technical sense, and was urged by Katrina not to dwell on the skills of reading, he was determined to make reading a fun experience for Marcus. He got a few MREs (meals ready-to-eat) food ration kits from a local Army reserve post and brought those to their sessions. As they sampled and snacked, they read *Alan's War: The Memories of G.I. Alan Cope* (Guibert, 2008). Written in prose accessible for Marcus, this graphic novel recounts the World War II experiences of Cope, who at 18 is shipped off to Europe.

As they read about Cope, Lionel informed Marcus about his own experiences as a young officer traveling to foreign countries, being exposed to new cultures, establishing enduring friendships. Cope speaks directly to the reader about his life in the military during wartime Europe from panels of gray, black, and white. They enjoyed the book so much that Lionel encouraged Marcus to work together to make their own graphic story, using the Cope graphic novel as an example. Marcus proved to be the much better illustrator, so Lionel helped with dialog and the storyline. They struck on the idea of drawing frames in which the two of them carry on a conversation about war, why they're fought, how they can be avoided. Along the way, Lionel worked with Marcus on sentence structure, word meanings, punctuation, and spelling.

In the first frame, for instance, Marcus's character asks Lionel's character the meaning of military intelligence. In the answer Lionel uses the words *encryption* and *cryptographer*. Marcus put words like these on flashcards, with the term on one side and definitional information on the other. Katrina gave them a toss-term box with clear plastic sleeves on each surface for holding vocabulary flashcards. At every session, new words were added. Lionel and Marcus would toss the box back and forth to review these words and quiz each other over pronunciation, meaning, and proper usage in a sentence. Once comfortable with his knowledge of a word, Lionel would have Marcus put the card in a separate stack of known words.

This same approach was used with another compelling graphic novel that Lionel and Marcus found in the school library. *Incognegro* (Johnson & Pleece, 2009) is the story of Zane Pinchback, an

African-American reporter for a New York newspaper, who because he is so light-skinned can pass for White. He goes undercover during the 1930s to investigate lynchings in the South. As African Americans, both Lionel and Marcus found the book exciting and powerful.

The book prompted numerous opportunities for conversation around race, prejudice, and identity, which Lionel capitalized on by using a threaded discussion much like a dialog journal. In it, Marcus would write his reaction to a scene or character from *Incognegro* and Lionel would respond with his own reactions. The librarian helped them set up a discussion board using Microsoft Outlook. After reading a section of the novel, they sat at adjacent terminals typing entries and responses back and forth. Lionel used this process to model questioning, writing in complete sentences, and critical thinking.

Reading *Incognegro* also led to reading about cases of racial prejudice in current events, such as anti-immigration policies in certain states of the United States, and the banning of Muslim head scarves in public in France. Marcus's strong reactions to the graphic novel and the other contemporary examples of racial prejudice gave Lionel the idea that he could express his opinions by writing to politicians. With Katrina's approval and help, Lionel worked with Marcus to write an appropriately styled letter in which he expressed his views about harsh anti-immigration laws, which their state's governor and attorney general supported. They made certain complete sentences were used, and grammar, punctuation, and spelling were correct. They found email addresses for the two officials and sent Marcus's letter as an attachment. Lionel wrote the cover email message, explaining his role in mentoring Marcus and how his letter came about. Katrina's only request was that Lionel use his own personal email address for correspondence. Within a couple of days, both the governor's and attorney general's offices sent appreciative replies that encouraged Marcus to continue to remain engaged in the political process. Although the replies were perfunctory, Marcus was happy to know he was able to communicate directly to politicians about his opinions.

Mentoring made a significant difference in the literate life of Marcus. As a result of his regular interactions with Lionel around engaging and accessible texts, Marcus expanded his word knowledge and reading capacities. He also discovered that reading could be pleasurable and informative. Lionel provided responsive literacy instruction by making sure the selection of texts and related literacy activities were in direct response to Marcus's interests and needs. Skills instruction was embedded within the context of enjoyable reading and meaningful communication experiences. Katrina was not surprised when results showed that Marcus's end-of-year reading test score had increased by 2 years, further demonstrating to her the added value of reading mentoring.

Teaching Basic Skills in Context to Students with Serious Reading Challenges

Finding the right balance of engaging text experiences and basic skills instruction for adolescents with very low reading levels and serious word recognition difficulties is, as Beers (2003) aptly points out, "difficult on good days, beyond frustrating on bad days" (p. 242). The typical response to students in this category is to put them into heavy-handed phonics programs or, as I suggested earlier in this chapter, reroute them through a regimen of basic skills instruction that failed to bring about improvement the first time. The problem with this response is that intensive phonics instruction has diminishing returns as students progress through the grades (National Reading Panel, 2000). Furthermore, even the staunchest advocates of phonics instruction have found that after the earliest phase of reading instruction it has little effect on increasing fluency or comprehension (Ehri, Nuves, Stahl, & Willows, 2001).

In my work as a literacy practicum supervisor, I have witnessed firsthand the consequences of a phonics-laden language arts curriculum for middle and upper grades students who are referred to our tutorial sites for reading services. When my graduate tutors conduct a diagnosis of these students they're often surprised to discover that they can *read* the assessment texts fairly well. That is, they can decode the words and read with some degree of expression and fluency. What these adolescents fail to possess, however, is the ability to *comprehend* what they have read. I have documented this strengthening pattern since No Child Left Behind was enacted, and teaching basic reading skills in schools became a national emphasis. One might say this emphasis has been largely successful, if most students are moving out of elementary school with strong decoding skills. Yet, without an equal emphasis on reading for meaning, our approaches to teaching reading to children will continue to produce competent word callers but weak meaning makers and critical thinkers.

The point is that for adolescents who may still need significant development in basic word recognition skills, approaches must stress contextual applications with real text that is engaging and accessible. Both fluency and word recognition can be improved through contextualized approaches, as explained in the following descriptions. Giving struggling adolescent readers immediate application of skills with text that informs and pleases will help them remain engaged instead of giving up, and build more confident and competent reading identities.

Fluency development in context. Helping students in the elementary grades become fluent readers is a goal of most reading programs. Fluency is considered one of the so-called five pillars of reading instruction as outlined in the National Reading Panel report. When this aspect of reading is an instructional emphasis, most young students learn to identify words with accuracy and appropriate speed, and apply these skills with proper phrasing and expression to text (Kuhn & Stahl, 2003).

An emphasis on fluency typically diminishes as students move from intermediate to middle grades and beyond (Rasinksi et al., 2005). Although some argue that fluency work with struggling adolescent readers can result in several benefits, including improved metacognition, an increase in confidence about reading skill, increased exposure to text, and the realization that ability improves with practice (Dudley, 2005).

Fluency—that is how accurately, rapidly, and with expression one reads a text—will depend on one's word recognition, print knowledge, and print experience skills (Hasbrouck & Tindal, 2006). The more automatic these fundamental reading skills are, the more cognitive energy is reserved for thinking about and comprehending text (Tractenberg, 2002). This may be of particular concern when negotiating disciplinary text with its expository text structures and complex concepts and terms. Text of this nature places a premium on deliberate and thoughtful reading. Consequently, students who recognize and can glide through most words in disciplinary text will have greater cognitive capacity for comprehension (Strong, Wehby, Falk, & Lane, 2004).

Because most youth develop appropriate automaticity with fluency-related skills by the time they reach middle and high school, curricular attention to fluency in language arts programs all but disappears. Nonetheless, some readers, such as English learners (Vaughn, Mathes, Linan-Thompson, & Francis, 2005) and learning disabled students (Archer, Gleason, & Vachon, 2003), may experience problems with accurate and quick decoding even as adolescents.

A simple truth about fluency is that, like other reading skills, it develops as a result of practice. For struggling adolescent readers, increasing fluency should not be an end goal in itself but a by-product of daily print experiences with accessible texts. Sustained, self-selected reading—an approach recommended earlier in this chapter for establishing a schoolwide literate culture—will be a critical element in improving fluency skills for all students, because we know that regular opportunities for recreational reading can have a measurable impact on comprehension as well as fluency (Krashen, 2004).

As indicated, increasing reading rate and automaticity for struggling middle and high school students is a worthwhile outcome of reading instruction, if for no other reason than the sheer volume of daily and weekly textbook reading typically required of secondary students. Homework reading assignments of even modest length in science, social studies, math, and literature could literally take several hours to complete; for very slow readers, more hours than they have after school and in the evening. Students who possess highly developed fluency skills will be able to drastically reduce reading time of complex disciplinary text.

Although there are no guarantees that struggling readers will become more enthusiastic about reading with work on increasing their fluency and automaticity, I have witnessed many students in our literacy practicum program exhibit greater self-efficacy and pride as they increase reading rate and become more fluent. The key is to ensure that improvement in fluency and comprehension occur simultaneously, so students realize that reading faster doesn't automatically mean reading better and that reading rate will be determined by one's purpose for reading.

A student's silent reading rate can be calculated with virtually any text. Rates can be recorded on a progress chart to give the student a graphic view of growth. The steps in Figure 3.7 will determine the words per minute (WPM) score. I recommend that struggling adolescent readers use accessible content-area text to practice increasing rate and automaticity. Ideally, texts should come from a student's independent reading level; in other words the kind of reading students can do on their own. Text from sources like Ben's Guide (http://bensguide.gpo.gov/) with easier passages on American history or Chem4Kids (www.chem4kids.com), a similar website in the area of science, math, and physics, allow students to increase fluency while gaining valuable knowledge of important content concepts and terms. Other good sources are the ancillary readings that accompany middle and high school textbooks. Companion readings to science, social studies, and math textbooks are particularly helpful for this purpose as they include high-interest passages written in a less textbook-like style.

Bearing in mind the point made earlier in this chapter concerning the limited benefits of phonics for older readers, I recommend these approaches for improving fluency.

1. Increase knowledge of high-frequency and sight words. Word knowledge and familiarity increase with exposure. It has been suggested that struggling readers and learners need two or three times as many exposures to words than those with normally developing vocabularies. Blevins (2001) asserts that a fraction of the total number of words in the English language account for most of the words

Figure 3.7. Steps in Calculating Words per Minute (WPM)

1. Count or estimate the number of words in a passage. For a short passage all the words can be counted. For longer passages, an average number of words per line can be multiplied by the total number of lines to derive an estimate of the overall word length.
2. Multiply the passage word length by 60. (Example: 400 word passage x 60 = 24000.)
3. The total time it takes for a student to read the 400-word passage is timed. A teacher or tutor can do the timing, or the student can time him/herself. (Example: total time = 120 seconds to read the 400 word passage.)
4. Divide the coefficient resulting from the passage word length multiplied by 60 by the total reading time to determine WPM. (Example: 24000 ÷ 120 = 200 WPM.)

found in printed text. Word lists, such as the Dolch Basic Sight Vocabulary and Fry's Instant Word List contain words that comprise perhaps as many as 50% of the words found in today's textbooks. Although these lists contain general vocabulary words, more complex terms appropriate to middle and upper grades students may be found in comprehensive lists, such as the ones found in *The Living Word Vocabulary* (Dale & O'Roarke, 1981), and those compiled for the academic subjects (Marzano & Pickering, 2005).

Students can rehearse manageable groups of words from these lists in short but frequent study sessions. In the practicum I supervise, I have students create toss-term boxes with clear plastic sleeves on each face of the box. In these sleeves index cards with high-frequency words, sight words, and common academic language terms are slotted. With their tutors or in small groups of students, the box is tossed and the word facing up to the one who catches the box must be pronounced correctly, defined, and put into a meaningful sentence. As words become familiar enough to be sight words, the index card can be pulled out replaced by new words.

2. Create opportunities for repeated readings of familiar text. Rereading is one of the best ways to improve fluency (Allington, 2009b; Samuels, 2002). Repeated reading has also been shown to increase comprehension, as student's reading becomes more automatic at the word level (Brozo, 1990; Cioffi & Carney, 1983).

With secondary-level students, I recommend using instructional level text for this purpose. I allow a student to read aloud for 1 to 3 minutes while recording miscues (i.e., any deviation from the text, including mispronunciations, word omissions, failure to attend to punctuation). Afterward, I go over the miscues and try to prompt instead of immediately providing the correct pronunciation. For example, I encourage the student to break words into recognizable parts, syllables, say the first part of the word, and use context to figure out the rest. In this way, the student can learn independent word recognition strategies.

Together we count the total number of words read correctly, divide by 60 (as in 60 seconds or 1 minute), and record this on a chart. I then ask the student to reread the same text at least two more times, paying particular attention to the miscues made previously as she or he strives to increase reading rate and accurate phrasing. With each repeated reading of the text, we correct miscues and record a new-words correct score on the chart. Documenting improvement in rate and accuracy is motivating to students.

With certain passages, I first model accurate reading and allow students to reread and rehearse them until they can deliver a near flawless oral rendition. This helps build self-confidence and pride.

3. Use echo and choral reading to model phrasing and intonation. Echo and choral reading are approaches that take advantage of the skills of the highly fluent reader (Gillet, Temple, & Crawford, 2008). Fluent reading of a text is modeled, and then the student either reads right behind or attempts to read in unison. Choral reading allows a teacher or tutor to work with a small group of students. These approaches have been shown to increase reading confidence as well as fluency (Padak & Rasinski, 2008).

4. Create opportunities for readers' theater that avoid stigmatizing struggling readers. In regards to these approaches to improving fluency and basic skills of older students, teachers and tutors need to be especially sensitive to how these practices may be perceived by adolescents. Even if a strategy has proven effectiveness with young readers, the same strategy may be stigmatizing to an older student who may have years of unsuccessful reading and learning experiences. Thus, while the text sources for developing these basic skills need to be accessible, they should not be "babyish" or recognized as such by the student and her or his peers.

Readers' theater approaches allow students to rehearse different parts of a text until fluency has been achieved. Then and only then are they invited to read their parts in a group format before an audience of the class or others. For example, when reading a class novel, students working on fluency could be allowed to rehearse independently the spoken parts of characters in an upcoming chapter, and then come together at the front of the room to give a readers' theater version. When finished, a new group of students could be called to the front to pick up where the previous group left off, and so on.

Developing word recognition skills in context. Although most students will develop word recognition skills in elementary school, we know that some students, especially those who are English learners, enter middle and high school without having developed a level expertise with these skills that's expected of them. For reasons already cited in this chapter, it is unlikely that isolated skill and drill approaches to teaching word recognition will yield positive results (Beers, 2003; Ivey & Baker, 2004). On the other hand, approaches that emphasize application of word recognition skills in context have the potential for helping striving readers increase comprehension (McCormick & Becker, 1996; Nagy, McLure, & Montserrat, 1997). After all, secondary-level students need to engage in as much authentic reading of disciplinary text as possible in order to gain information and knowledge (Shanahan & Shanahan, 2008; Stanovich & Cunningham, 1993).

Adolescents with seriously underdeveloped word recognition skills and strategies may need a number of accommodations in order to increase their capacity. First among these is to teach word recognition in context with text that is accessible. If too many words are unrecognizable, there will not be enough context to make instruction in this strategy worthwhile. Less challenging texts for readers in these situations is critical so they can maximize cognitive effort on learning word recognition strategies (Brozo & Afflerbach, 2011).

Typical of older students with limited word recognition skill is the tendency to make guesses at words while reading instead of limiting the possibilities by using sentence and paragraph contexts. For example, Javier, a struggling 8th-grader, often would not attend to the middles of words. He might say "great" for *graduate* or "common" for *competition*. To force Javier to attend to semantic clues during word recognition instruction, target words were partially clozed, as in the case below with an accessible text on the American Civil War:

Word: *Confederate*

Context: *The Union soldiers marched up the rugged mountain trail the entire day, then made camp on the summit. The wide open view into the valley below offered the perfect lookout on the advancing* <u>Con ate</u> *army.*

Repeatedly drawing Javier's attention to the way context, with its semantic and syntactic clues, restricts plausible options for words not immediately recognized armed him with a new and useful independent reading strategy.

A more involved approach that nonetheless capitalizes on authentic contexts for recognizing words was practiced by a 9th-grade low-track English teacher with a group of struggling readers. The teacher quickly realized a workbook approach to teaching word families around consonant blends was not only failing to produce transfer to real reading, but was also turning her students off to reading altogether. After reading some journal articles and consulting with colleagues, she devised an alternative instructional strategy for teaching word families with /ch/ and /ck/ sounds.

The approach took advantage of the youths' own media. First, she invited students to bring to class song lyrics from their favorite musical artists. The lyrics had to be free of profanity and sexism. Students brought everything from rap to country. Next, students looked through the lyrics and pulled out all words that conformed to the two consonants.

With the American rapper Snoop Dogg's lyrics for "I Love to Give You Light," a couple of students found numerous examples of words with /ch/ and /ck/ blends. These words were written into a t-chart in their vocabulary notebooks (see Figure 3.8).

Figure 3.8. T-Chart for /ch/ and /ck/ Words in Snoop Dogg's "I Love to Give You Light"

ch	ck
choir	background
such	jackers
alchemist	glock
preach	block
church	locked
teachin	black
watchin	**socks**
each	**backpack**
preachin	**locker**
reach	
purchase	
Beach	
child	
catch	

The students continued working together to brainstorm new words with the /ch/ and /ck/ sounds and add them to the t-chart. Finally, student pairs wrote their own lyrics based on the genre they brought to class. The lyrics had to contain all or some of the new words they generated for the two word families.

Students working with the Snoop Dogg lyrics wrote a rap. As one student read the rap the other kept rhythm on his desk top:

> *I put my **socks** in my **backpack** when I go to school. I put my **backpack** in my **locker** or I look like a fool. I get my **socks** from my **backpack** when I go to gym. Where I **catch** the ball then stick it in the rim.*

Based on this activity, the students were much more aware of words with the /ch/ and /ck/ blends and became skillful at recognizing them in their reading and writing. This approach to teaching word recognition skills was successful for two reasons. First, it eliminated barriers between students' outside-of-school texts and classroom practices, which increased engagement in learning (Sturtevant, Boyd, Brozo, Hinchman, Alvermann, & Moore, 2006). Second, it demonstrated for these striving readers that basic reading skills can be applied to texts in their everyday worlds (Harmon, 2002).

CHAPTER SUMMARY

Helping adolescent readers, especially those who are struggling, develop levels of reading and writing competence necessary for academic learning is a demanding task, regardless of the approach or program. To be successful, a total commitment is required of all teachers and teacher leaders. Growth may not always be as rapid as hoped but is far more likely to occur when secondary teachers, administrators, and support staff dedicate themselves to responsive and culturally sensitive practices for all readers.

Since an RTI-like approach to address the literacy needs of secondary students is not written into law and has been under-explored and implemented in middle and high school, it should be regarded as one option among many. Thus, in this chapter I proposed that RTI be reframed as responsive literacy instruction guided by principles that honor adolescent identity as well as the complexities of literacy learning in secondary school.

As you reflect on the ideas and practices discussed in this chapter, consider the approaches you might use to prevent reading and learning difficulties from developing, and responsive literacy interventions you might employ for struggling readers and learners. As you do, remember that these students will need the best of what we know about literacy and youth culture. They will need engaging and meaningful strategies that expand interest, build competence, and promote a sense of agency and independence. They will need highly knowledgeable and skillful teachers as well as comprehensive literacy programs that offer opportunities for encounters with multiple texts and forms of representation throughout the school day. And, perhaps most critically, striving readers will need teachers and school personnel interested in forming close and supportive relationships with them as a context for literacy and learning growth.

Relate to Integrate

Whether you are working individually or with a group of others, take a few moments to reflect on the chapter you have just read. To facilitate your learning, consider the following:

1. Highlight the differences between responsive instruction and intervention.

Individual: Write a journal reflection that highlights the differences between responsive instruction and intervention.

Group: Have each participant write differences on sticky notes. Participants take turns putting their sticky notes up and sharing thoughts. Facilitator will lead discussion.

2. Apply the five principles of responsive literacy instruction:

1. Views adolescents as a resource.
2. Occurs within comprehensive literacy programs.
3. Provides special supports, but not always special settings.
4. Includes more than a curriculum of basic skills.
5. Comes from effective teachers who have the knowledge and practices to address struggling adolescent readers' needs.

Individual: Reflect on your own practice and think about how you can integrate these five principles in your practice.

Group: Have each participant make a Stop Doing List, a list of practices that they believe do not support the five principles of responsive literacy instruction. Participants should pair with a partner, combine lists, and share out.

3. Create an instrument to acquire feedback on student literacy/learning.
Review the four methods of assessing literacy cloze/maze passage, vocabulary self-assessment, vocabulary matching, and bubble maps.

Individual: Use your own classroom materials to create an instrument using one or more of the assessment methods.

Group: Work with a partner to create an instrument using one or more of the assessment methods. Share your ideas with another pair.

4. How does your school culture support literacy?

Individual: Take 3 minutes to jot down a quick list of ways that your school culture supports literacy. Take an additional 3 minutes to jot down things that you wish your school would do to support literacy.

Group: Take 3 minutes to jot down a quick list of ways that your school culture supports literacy. Take an additional 3 minutes to jot down things that you wish your school would do to support literacy. Share with the group in facilitator-lead discussion.

CHAPTER 4

RTI for Secondary Literacy: Analysis of School Cases

HIGHLIGHTS

- Case descriptions of three secondary schools/systems applying RTI practices serve as a focus for analysis based on the five principles of responsive literacy instruction presented in Chapter 3.
- When actual principles of responsive adolescent literacy instruction are considered, current secondary RTI approaches can all be strengthened by aligning practices with youths' academic, motivational, and identity needs.

I HAVE PREMISED THIS BOOK on the reality that RTI for literacy is principally an approach reserved for students at the primary and elementary levels. And even here, the jury is still out as to whether RTI can produce the kinds of outcomes envisioned by its advocates (Allington, 2008). Fully operational RTI approaches for secondary school literacy with demonstrable success are rare. Those who have attempted to implement RTI in middle and high school settings have few examples from the upper grades to guide them. As I argued in Chapter 2, the complexity of secondary school institutions and culture, as well as the complexities of adolescence mean that most examples of RTI at the primary and elementary levels are of little use as guides to how to do RTI for older students (Goetze, Laster, & Ehren, 2010).

In this chapter I foreground three existing cases of RTI being implemented in some form at the secondary level. These cases from U.S. middle and high schools were selected because they represent different regions of the country and different demographics: a small community, a midsized city, and a large, culturally diverse metropolitan area. Another important criterion for a school's inclusion was that the RTI approach was ongoing and had been in place for 2 or more years, or long enough for at least some data on its effectiveness to have been acquired.

The description of each school's approach to RTI is summarized in a manner similar to the *RTI in the Real World* features that appear in Chapters 1, 2, 3, and 5. The description is based on information available at the school's website, conversations and interviews with key school personnel responsible for initiating and overseeing RTI, and a school visit (Case #1). For each school, I provide a critical analysis guided by the five principles of responsive literacy instruction presented in Chapter 3:

- Responsive literacy instruction views adolescents as a resource
- Responsive literacy instruction occurs within comprehensive literacy programs
- Responsive literacy instruction provides special supports but not always special settings
- Responsive literacy instruction includes more than a curriculum of basic skills redux

- Responsive literacy instruction comes from effective teachers who have the knowledge and practices to address struggling adolescent readers' needs

My intent for this analysis is not to be polemical but to take a considered look at key components of RTI as it is being implemented in these particular secondary school cases. Therefore, within the analysis, I make suggestions for alternative ways of thinking about the cases and offer ways of improving features of each school's approaches to make them more responsive to youths' literacy needs.

ANALYSIS OF SCHOOL CASES OF RTI FOR SECONDARY LITERACY

Case #1
Liberty Middle School, Hanover County, Virginia

Since implementing a leveled intervention program, Liberty Middle School (LMS), nestled in rolling farmland outside of Ashland, Virginia, has experienced significant gains in reading as well as a sizeable reduction in the number of students being referred for special education services. In 2004, LMS received a 3-year grant to partner with the University of Kansas and the state of Virginia to implement the Content Literacy Continuum® (CLC). Since implementing the program, an additional 5-year grant was awarded through a state improvement grant. The gains made in this rural, Hanover County, Virginia school have benefitted a diverse population of approximately 1,100 students. The population is comprised of 82.6% Caucasian, 14.6% African American, and 2.8% Hispanic students, with 27.2% of the total population receiving free or reduced lunches.

The program adopted by LMS, the Content Literacy Continuum® (CLC), is a five-level intervention program. The CLC levels compare to RTI tiers with CLC levels 1 and 2 being analogous to Tier 1; levels 3 and 4 paralleling Tier 2; and levels 3, 4, and 5 being similar to Tier 3 interventions in the RTI process. In the CLC model, there is overlap between each level, as well as different stages within each level. Within a given level, all teachers embed content-literacy strategies (stage A) but also cue appropriate strategies for students who need additional support (stage B). At the heart of the CLC program is data-driven decision making and ongoing professional development centered on the Strategic Instruction Model® (SIM). The key components of the SIM approach include teacher instructional routines and student learning strategies.

At Liberty Middle School, the CLC program was executed in four overlapping phases: exploring, planning, implementing, and sustaining. During the summer-long exploration phase, the site needs were assessed. Once the needs were recognized, a plan for the identification and development of teacher leaders and professional developers was prepared. The ongoing implementation was described as a feedback model of evolution; Liberty Middle School is now entering the sustaining phase of the program. In the beginning phases, the professional developers and teacher leaders were considered the infrastructure of the program and played a pivotal role in promoting teacher buy-in and building capacity at the school. Beginning in August of 2005, teachers began Strategic Instruction Model® (SIM) Professional Development (PD), focusing on Content Enhancement Routines (CER) and Learning Strategies (LS). CER PD was targeted for levels 1 and 2 teachers, and LS training was intended for levels 3, 4, and 5 teachers. In CLC training is ongoing; teachers and other instructional professionals are scheduled to participate in training 3 to 4 times per year in order to meet the changing needs of the school.

Because the professional development needs are constantly changing, training is adjusted to meet those needs by building on the initial CER and LS PD. At LMS, the CER PD has centered on course organizer, unit organizer, framing, concept mastery, LINCing, and survey routines. For LS PD the focus and participants differ according to the intervention level, with more intensive applications of the strategies occurring at the higher levels. LS PD has included specific strategy instruction on sentence writing, paraphrasing, inference, first-letter mnemonic, and test-taking strategies. Professional development at the higher intensity levels, which focuses on foundational skills, have included instruction in the Wilson Reading program and Read 180®. At the highest intervention level PD for the speech and language pathologist is focused on delivering individualized curriculum-relevant therapies. As implementation has progressed, additional CERs and LSs have been added to the professional development curriculum and have included items such as formative assessments and disciplinary literacy. Supplementary training on additional routines and strategies has been offered on a voluntary basis throughout the program. The overall goal of the professional development has been to embed CERs and LSs into daily instruction for all students at all levels.

To ensure that each classroom employs the SIM approach, administrators were charged with building a culture that would support CLC and become familiar with the SIM CERs and LSs. Administrator knowledge of the CERs and LSs is important in order to facilitate the monitoring process. The monitoring process encompasses repeated classroom observations, which are termed *walk-throughs*, and are regularly scheduled to allow observations of SIM implementation during various parts of classroom instruction. As the implementation process has matured, a data collection component and a fidelity check have been added to the walk-through routine. The information gathered from the walk-throughs has been used, and continues to be used, to make professional development decisions.

Coaches are an integral part of the professional development program; they serve as the bridge between training and integrating the CERs and LSs into practice. Throughout implementation of the program, certified SIM coaches have worked with all instructional personnel providing individual, small-group, and department-level support. To ensure sustainability, four LMS teachers were identified early on to become certified SIM professional developers, who later assumed the role of coaches within the school. Liberty Middle School now has all in-house coaches who have enhanced the collaborative work environment at the school. Teachers eagerly sign up for opportunities to participate in coaching activities that include common planning time, in house video of SIM strategies at work, and collegial teaching groups.

Placement of students at the appropriate level is important to the success of the CLC program. At LMS the universal screening tool is the Scholastic Reading Inventory (SRI), a computer-based reading assessment that is given three times per year to monitor student progress. Students are identified for interventions based on data from the prior 2 years, SRI scores, standardized test performance, and benchmark assessment performance. Student math and reading data are reviewed four times per year (in August, October, January, and February/March) and in science twice per year, in order to assess whether changes to student's intervention levels are needed. In addition to the SRI data, formative assessments, which are contained within each of the CERs, allow teachers to identify students who require more intensive instructional support. The type of support that is available is dependent on the level at which the student is performing.

The CLC process at LMS has entailed a cultural shift and a recursive progression of identifying professional development needs by means of administrative walk-throughs, CLC sweeps, and coaching. The school continues in this progression, with each component serving a key purpose in the evolutionary feedback loop. As the process has progressed, the data collected from the walk-throughs and the CLC sweeps have identified future professional development and coaching needs that serve as conduits by which the entire process can be refined to meet current and future school needs. The school underwent a cultural shift, from an environment of evaluation to one of support, one that was attributed to the coaching component of the program, in which teachers eagerly participate. As the school approaches the sustaining phase, administration is focused on adding a behavioral management component to the program.

Analysis of Case #1

Responsive literacy instruction views adolescents as a resource. There is no evidence that students from Liberty Middle School were brought into a conversation about the Content Literacy Continuum® (CLC), either during the planning stages or in any ongoing way. As was pointed out in the previous chapter, adolescent readers, including those who are struggling, are often quite capable of articulating the nature of their challenges with literacy and, indeed, what teachers and others might do to support them (Brozo, 2006a). Although it's true that teachers at LMS are gathering data on students in a regular and systematic way, these sources of information are based on assessments and classroom assignments and not built around direct student input into their own reading and learning interests, skills, and challenges.

Liberty Middle could sponsor an advisory group comprised of students from a range of ability levels. The group could offer input in areas such as how to increase motivation for reading, structuring school time for recreational reading, teacher supports for students having difficulty with the class textbook reading, and classroom activities to make content reading and learning interesting. Faculty, administrators, and support staff could find ways of integrating students' suggestions into daily instructional routines around the CLC approach.

In schools like LMS where programs have been adopted, in the case of the CLC, there is an explicit agreement between the school and the exporter of the program that fidelity to its assessment and instructional guidelines be maintained. RTI devotees stress the importance of teachers employing only evidence-based practices to ensure consistency and fidelity. The language of evidence-based practice comes directly from IDEA. However, when students are invited into a discussion about how to increase their own reading engagement and achievement, their ideas may not fit neatly into evidence-based routines. Nonetheless, these student-derived suggestions may have just as much potential for preventing reading and learning difficulties and improving progress for struggling readers.

Responsive literacy instruction occurs within comprehensive literacy programs. Because every teacher at LMS has been provided training and is expected to deliver SIM instructional routines and learning strategies, there is a schoolwide feel to the five-level approach to content literacy interventions. Liberty Middle School also has off-the-shelf intervention options for students including the Wilson Reading and READ 180.

An added dimension to SIM strategies and the other programs at LMS would be a schoolwide approach to encouraging independent reading for the young adolescents. With such a strong emphasis on strategic reading, students at LMS would undoubtedly benefit from daily sustained reading, especially as we know there is a close relationship between regular print encounters, reading engagement, and reading achievement for adolescents (Brozo, Shiel, & Topping, 2007/2008).

Responsive literacy instruction provides special supports but not always special settings. There is an emphasis on prevention of student reading and writing difficulties at LMS, as evidenced by the push to train every teacher in the use of content-enhancement routines and learning strategies. Moreover, teachers are monitored and provided additional support to ensure these instructional strategies become integrated within daily lessons. Evidence suggests that this school-wide effort contributed to a significant decline in special education referrals over the past 3 years. This means the reading, writing, and learning strategies general education teachers are embedding in their lessons are helping students who might otherwise be moved out of the classroom, remain with their peers and make adequate progress. This is critical, because once students are placed in alternative settings for instruction, their return may not be easy or timely.

Liberty Middle's success in limiting referrals of students for special learning supports might be enhanced with other initiatives. Instead of pulling students out of the general education classroom, a special teacher support time could be established that allows struggling students to receive individualized attention on actual curricular materials and content (Gregory & Kuzmich, 2005). Sometimes referred to as a Student Assistance Period (SAP), it might occur during homeroom time or some other 25- to 30-minute opening during the school day. Student Assistance Period has been more feasible in schools with block scheduling, like that at Liberty Middle. During SAP, all classroom and support teachers remain in their classrooms to receive individual students who go to them for assistance. This dedicated time for student assistance is spent re-teaching, providing alternative explanations and learning experiences, and giving students additional guided practice (Goetze, Laster, & Ehren, 2010). Struggling readers and learners can be required to attend SAP and maintain a log as part of a contract for improvement.

Responsive literacy instruction includes more than a curriculum of basic skills redux. Students with low scores on the SRI and other initial placement measures at LMS may find themselves receiving interventions in the form of the Wilson Reading system and/or READ 180.

Wilson Reading was originally designed to teach adult dyslexics and follows the Orton multisensory approach. It is recommended only for students who have serious difficulties decoding and spelling (Deschler, Palincsar, Biancarosa, & Nair, 2007). In essence, Wilson is an intensive, systematic phonics program for individuals and small groups of students with similar levels of reading ability. Although some evidence suggests the program can benefit older struggling readers (Florida Center for Reading Research, 2006), it must be regarded as an intervention of last resort for adolescent readers, and only one facet of an array of interventions. Furthermore, as Ivey and Baker (2004) have convincingly pointed out, struggling adolescent readers have more than likely been through a regimen of basic skills instruction once, twice, or multiple years with no significant effect on achievement.

Thus, LMS students who exhibit very low performance on the standardized test of reading will also need opportunities for extended and sustained print experiences (Krashen, 2004), with embedded and contextualized skill development. Frequent encounters with modified and accessible disciplinary text will be critical to building knowledge along with skill. To buoy these students' motivation, which is often as depressed as their achievement, they could work with cross-age tutors and community mentors, as I recommended in Chapter 3.

READ 180 was probably selected as an intervention program because it is designed to be delivered in a 90-minute period, the schedule LMS introduced when the CLC approach was launched. The rationale is that a block schedule accommodates the extra time classroom teachers need to embed new instructional routines and strategies into their lessons. Instruction typically comes in the form of teacher whole group instruction for 30 minutes, followed by small group and independent work, then concluding whole group activities with the teacher. The middle school version of READ 180 includes support of activities and skill building more in line with what most struggling young adolescent readers will need, such as opportunities for independent reading, software-based individualized instruction in academic vocabulary, comprehension, writing, and study reading with fiction and nonfiction.

One might argue, given the extent of teacher involvement in READ 180 and the focus on academic vocabulary and reading comprehension, that the approach could be integrated within every LMS teachers' instructional plan so that students apply word learning and strategic reading directly to the texts they encounter daily. This could eliminate the expense of and the need for a special program and separate instructional setting.

I have one final cautionary note about off-the-shelf programs for reading intervention. When LMS or any school incurs the expense of these costly and often involved systems, they are going to get used. However, the struggling readers assigned to these programs may or may not see their achievement increase. This is because in spite of a seal of approval by RTI proponents and the so-called scientific basis for the products, Wilson and READ 180 can never deliver truly responsive literacy instruction to each individual student. Only a caring and knowledgeable teacher can.

Responsive literacy instruction comes from effective teachers who have the knowledge and practices to address struggling adolescent readers' needs. Perhaps the strongest aspect of the CLC approach in place at LMS is teacher professional development (PD). Professional development was frontloaded before and during the launch of the new reading and writing initiatives and is ongoing. This is not to say that PD has been uniformly embraced. Like most secondary schools, the teaching culture at LMS has presented administrators and professional developers the challenge of ensuring fidelity of strategic instruction across disciplines. Administrator walk-throughs could be regarded as de facto evidence of the struggle to get total buy-in by classroom teachers. However, monitoring of CLC activity is meant to uncover aspects of the program that could be improved through customized PD.

One indication of the potential effectiveness of PD at LMS is the sharp decline in special education referrals. To what extent this has occurred as a result of admonishments by administrators to reduce such referrals or through PD that has raised the capacity level of teachers to address the literacy and learning needs of all students, cannot be known from the existing case data. What is more, PD at LMS is focused exclusively on CLC strategies and not other adolescent literacy practices, such as exploiting youths' expertise with outside-of-school literacies and promoting critical reading of electronic texts. Nonetheless, teachers have received and continue to receive PD that would seem to be forcing reflection on practice and in recognition that change occurs for different teachers at different times (Dozier, 2006).

Case #2
Lincoln Public Schools, Lincoln, Nebraska

Lincoln, Nebraska is a midsize city of about a quarter of a million citizens in the heartland of the United States. Lincoln Public Schools are in the 2nd year of implementation of a secondary RTI program in 10 middle schools, which serve grades 6 through 8 in Lincoln, Nebraska. The focus of the RTI program is to improve literacy by providing below-level readers with research-based interventions. Preliminary evidence indicates a marked improvement in performance on the Test of Reading Comprehension (TORC), a commercially available silent reading test, and Test of Written Language (TOWL), a diagnostic writing assessment, as well as a slight drop in the number of students being referred to special education for learning disabilities and/or speech-language impairment since implementing the RTI program.

Students are placed in the appropriate intervention tiers based on universal screening data. These data are collected from achievement results on the Iowa Test of Basic Skills (ITBS), classroom reading and writing assessments, performance on statewide assessments, and report card scores. Before students enter the 6th grade, their reading achievement data are examined to ensure appropriate placement in the RTI process. Student performance data from the ITBS in the areas of reading fluency and comprehension, the 4th-grade results of the Nebraska State Writing Test (NeSA-W), and student report cards are closely scrutinized to make determinations about the match between student needs and the RTI program. Although data are first examined at the district level, the final decision is made by the school principals, instructional coordinators, and special education coordinators at the individual school level.

Lincoln Public Schools invested heavily in the initial professional development phase of the program by providing the middle school teachers, speech-language pathologists, and psychologists an intensive 3-day summer program that focused on research-based classroom interventions. The reading intervention training focused on specific interventions in the areas of reading fluency, vocabulary, comprehension of expository and narrative text, syntax, and writing. In the area of fluency, teachers were taught interventions for repeated reading and reading phrasing. In the area of vocabulary, teachers were given instruction on strategies for teaching targeted words in narrative and expository texts as well as prefix and root word instruction. In the construct of reading comprehension, teachers were trained on teaching syntax, reciprocal teaching, interactive reading, text structure and organization, identifying main ideas, and making inferences. In writing, teachers were given strategy instruction in sentence expansion, transformational grammar, and the use of graphic organizers for generating summary paragraphs.

Ongoing professional development is referred to as the application and problem-solving phase. It is designed to help teachers put the reading interventions into action and to instruct teachers in analyzing the formative assessment data they collect to guide their instructional decisions for grouping and regrouping students for re-teaching when needed. Professional development is offered five times per year. Districtwide, the teachers convene to discuss problems, fine tune intervention strategies, add new strategies, and examine data on DIBELS (Dynamic Indicators of Basic Early Literacy Skills), the AIMSWEB-MAZE probe data, and writing prompt data. A new dimension that has been added is the videotaping of the strategies in action to provide a model of good instruction for all teachers. RTI para-educators are assigned to the Tier 2 RTI class and are responsible for scoring and recording summative assessments and formative progress-monitoring data, and assisting students in the application of the reading strategies.

Currently the Tier 1 professional development focus is on struggling writers, guided reading groups, and differentiated instruction. Literacy support staff includes literacy coaches and speech-language pathologists. The primary responsibility of the support staff is to assist Tier 1 teachers in applying reading strategies within their classrooms.

Tier 1. The Tier 1 interventions occur in the general education classrooms, primarily in the English and language arts classrooms. The target size of these classrooms is 25 to 30 students. The content-area teachers have been given training in differentiating instruction and effective instructional strategies. Support staff is available to the teachers to assist in the application of appropriate strategies to the whole group or small groups within the classroom.

Tier 2. When entering 6th grade, students who are reading at the 3rd- or 4th-grade level, reading at least 70 words correctly per minute, performing within the 1st quartile of the ITBS, not passing the 4th-grade NeSA-W; and who show substandard performance in reading fluency, reading comprehension, and writing as indicated on the 5th-grade student report card, are recommended for placement in the Tier 2 RTI intervention. Students who are in the Tier 2 intervention program continue to receive the Tier 1 core instruction.

The Tier 2 RTI class size is between 12 and 15 students. Students meet every day for one full period, approximately 50 minutes. Tier 2 students are required to use one of their exploratory elective periods for Tier 2 interventions. The Tier 2 classrooms are staffed with a part-time trained para-educator available to assist the teacher and school psychologist with weekly progress monitoring and scoring and recording of the data.

Progress monitoring is performed weekly by the intervention team. The process begins with DIBELS and AIMSWEBB-MAZE testing performed during the first week of the cycle and writing, prompts given during the 2nd week of the cycle. The monitoring is repeated weekly with each cycle being performed biweekly. Test results are shared weekly with students during individual student conferences. Students participate in setting goals for themselves for the next 2 weeks. Data are reviewed continuously to determine if re-teaching or regrouping is needed. Data are reviewed quarterly to determine if students are ready to exit the program.

Additionally at Tier 2, two computer-based programs, READ 180 and System 44™, are being piloted with struggling readers to assist in literacy instruction. The READ 180 program also used by Liberty Middle School, was described above. System 44 similar to Wilson Reading, and also used in Liberty Middle's CLC program, focuses on foundational reading skills, decoding, and phonics.

Tier 3. Students receiving special education services are served in Tier 3. Identification for Tier 3 is warranted when the progress monitoring data do not indicate that the student is making adequate gains with the Tier 1 and Tier 2 supports.

Analysis of Case #2

Responsive literacy instruction views adolescents as a resource. Literacy instruction can only truly be considered responsive to the needs of youth if it honors their culture, experiences, and insights into their own reading and learning. The case information for Lincoln Schools does not allow for any clear generalizations about whether instruction for struggling readers includes consideration of their background experience and self-assessments. However, within the context of the RTI assessments for progress monitoring in Lincoln Schools, individual students conference with teachers and paraprofessionals on a weekly basis to reflect on the results and set achievement goals for the following 2 weeks.

Although restricted to the narrowly focused assessment-based goals of RTI, this may be, nonetheless, as close as it gets to encouraging student buy-in to the reading development approach in Lincoln. Yet, adolescents need much more to stay motivated and to build reading competencies. Guthrie (1996) has warned that achievement gains outside the intervention context may not occur when students:

> read merely to complete an assignment, with no sense of involvement of curiosity, they are being compliant. They conform to the demands of the situation irrespective of their personal goals. Compliant students are not likely to become lifelong learners. (p. 433)

One way to keep struggling middle graders motivated to read is to create numerous reading opportunities with relevant and accessible print and electronic sources (Alvermann, 2002).

Responsive literacy instruction occurs within comprehensive literacy programs. Here, too, case information on Lincoln Schools is not full enough to know whether behind RTI activity other schoolwide initiatives to promote literacy growth for all students are present. As I indicated in Chapter 1, RTI approaches with their heavy emphasis on learning/reading disabled students once adopted by a middle or high school tends to reinforce the already entrenched idea among many secondary-level teachers and administrators that literacy development resources for adolescents need only be directed toward those who are struggling. And when RTI consumes a large share of the energies of school personnel and its financial resources, there is little time or money left for other critical components of a comprehensive secondary literacy program, such as promoting wide- and regular-reading, increasing reading engagement, and building reading competence with complex disciplinary texts.

Lincoln Schools' inclusion of READ 180 and System 44 are reserved for Tier 2 students, and should only be considered pieces of a comprehensive literacy approach. As Fisher and Ivey point out:

> Older students need to "see the big picture" when it comes to reading and writing, and good interventions should begin with reading, writing, listening to, and thinking about meaningful texts. Instruction in the processes of reading and writing (e.g., word recognition, comprehension strategies, vocabulary, fluency) ought to help facilitate student engagement and understanding with real texts rather than take center stage in the program. (2006, pp. 182–183)

Lincoln could institute schoolwide approaches to increasing students' print encounters with texts that are meaningful to them. They might also recruit community volunteers as mentors to spend time with students reading and writing around authentic text.

Responsive literacy instruction provides special supports but not always special settings. The structure and process of RTI for middle schools in the Lincoln district most closely resemble approaches typical of their primary and elementary level counterparts. There is universal screening for initial placement, three tiers of intervention, and progress monitoring. I have asserted repeatedly that RTI should be considered one possible response to the injunctions in IDEA that call for reading and learning prevention and intervention. At the same time, I have made clear that in the absence of effective RTI-like approaches for literacy at the secondary level, middle and high schools are left to their own devices to create a prevention/intervention system. Thus, we see how Lincoln is attempting to appropriate an elementary school approach with little variation for its middle schools.

Ideally, tiered services are cascading, so students who are found to need Tier 2 and Tier 3 supports continue to receive instruction with their peers in Tier 1, the general education classroom. At Lincoln this seems to hold true, at least for students who find themselves in need of Tier 2 services. This compounding of instruction as opposed to displacing general education for special instructional services is preferred, but comes at a price to the student and is indicative of the challenges proponents of RTI encounter when trying to fit an approach more suited structurally to the elementary grades into the complex, departmentalized world of middle school. Tier 2 students at Lincoln must give up an elective course for extra reading assistance, because there is no room in the students' schedules. This solution may make sense to the architects of the RTI system, but it fails to acknowledge the motivational aspects of student choice, especially for young adolescents whose elective course may be the last reason to stay in school.

Students who fail to make adequate progress in spite of Tier 1 and 2 interventions, can find themselves in Tier 3 settings at Lincoln, the most sequestered of the learning environments. Students are likely to remain in Tier 3 at least for a quarter, as that is when student achievement is reassessed for placement decisions.

Teachers with whom I have worked discovered the benefits of pairing a struggling reader with a successful one within the classroom. This approach has shown the most promise when there is a gender and culture match (Zirkel, 2002). For example, when 13-year-old Hector, a recent immigrant from Honduras, came into his 7th-grade science class, the teacher invited another of her Hispanic male students, Miguel, to work with him. Miguel had immigrated with his family to the United States when he was a child, but spoke fluent Spanish. He was also one of her high achievers. Miguel's interactions and informal tutoring of Hector helped accelerate his progress as a reader and learner in science.

Responsive literacy instruction includes more than a curriculum of basic skills redux. Since 2000 and the release of the National Reading Panel's report and the enactment of NCLB a couple of years later, beginning reading programs in American schools have become decidedly skills-based. As the supervisor of a graduate school reading practicum, I have witnessed firsthand the effects a skills-emphasis reading curriculum has on older students. I take our program out to schools to work with struggling readers. Most middle-grades students who come for literacy tutoring demonstrate competence with foundational reading skills, such as phonics, phonemic awareness, and fluency, because that is what was emphasized in their elementary reading programs. Confounding to my graduate literacy tutors is that these same students have difficulty comprehending the texts they read.

I mention this to reinforce the point I've made before that older students who struggle with reading do not necessarily need another pass through a basic skills program. And yet, basic skills assessments and instruction have a prominent place in the Lincoln middle schools RTI approach, as evidenced by its use of DIBELS and System 44. DIBELS is supposed to provide a measure of phonemic awareness by asking students to pronounce as quickly as possible a list of nonsense syllables. It was initially intended to be one small piece of an overall assessment composite. However, critics have pointed out that DIBELS has been used to fashion whole-reading curricula around this ability to decode nonsense words, a skill that has little or no correlation to reading comprehension (Goodman, 2006). Moreover, DIBELS was designed with beginning readers in mind, and was never intended to extend to the upper grades. This last point is particularly relevant to secondary-level students whose primary challenge is learning how to read and learn from disciplinary text.

As for System 44, this is an off-the-shelf program designed to build foundational reading skills, such as phonics and phonemic awareness, so it fits neatly with a DIBELS approach to assessment. The publisher boasts that the age-appropriate adaptive technology of the program will motivate students who have become disenfranchised after years of academic failure. What is just as possible, however, is that adolescents assigned to this program might become even more disillusioned and demotivated (Fisher & Ivey, 2006; O'Brien, 2001).

Responsive literacy instruction comes from effective teachers who have the knowledge and practices to address struggling adolescent readers' needs. There appear to be two ways in which teacher input plays a meaningful role in the RTI process in Lincoln middle schools. First, although placement decisions rely heavily on standardized test results from such instruments as the Iowa Test of Basic Skills and the Nebraska State Writing Test, teachers' classroom assessments of reading and writing and their grades are factored into the decision making about which tier of intervention may be best for each student. Whether teacher judgment is trumped by standardized test scores cannot be determined from the case information, but that their input is included at all is a positive aspect of the Lincoln system (Alvermann & Rush, 2004). Teachers' insights into the needs of struggling middle grades readers, based on their daily interactions with them, should be given primacy over test data as decisions are made about the best ways to improve the literacy growth (Johnston, 1987).

Another significant way teachers are brought into the RTI process in Lincoln is through professional development (PD). Because middle graders move from classroom to classroom throughout the day to receive instruction from as many as six or seven different teachers, every faculty member should be as highly skilled as possible in the delivery of prevention and intervention strategies, if RTI is to be effective for all students. There is no real substitute for effective teaching (Flynt & Brozo, 2009), especially when it comes to struggling readers, who improve as a result of extensive interaction with expert teachers (Ivey, 1999a; McCormick, 1994; Morris, Ervin, & Conrad, 1996).

Case #3
San Diego Unified School District, San Diego, California

The San Diego Unified School District in San Diego, California is the 8th largest district in the United States. Highly diverse, nearly one-third of its students are English Language Learners.

The San Diego school district has teamed with the University of California, Berkeley on a U.S. Department of Education IES grant to implement the Striving Readers project. Launched in 2006, the project is designed to increase students' reading achievement as they progressed from grades 7 through 10. Students are considered eligible for targeted intervention based on cutoff scores from any one of three tests: the Degrees of Reading Power (DRP), the California English Language Development Test (CELDT), or the California Standards Test-English Language Arts (CST-ELA). During the Year 1 pilot study, two high schools and three middle schools participated; in Year 2, this expanded to the intended four high and four middle schools, for a total of 600 students assigned to the targeted interventions (out of a total of 6,300 students at the eight schools). Students who exceed the cutoff scores on the designated eligibility tests are assigned to elective classes during the reading intervention time, but are still part of the whole-school intervention, and still take the required language arts classes.

Content teachers from the middle and high schools were expected to complete approximately 200 hours of professional development. This included a 2-day introductory workshop, 3 full days of follow-up training, monthly meetings between district staff and teachers, and four discussion sessions between teachers and developers at each school. The school district also has provided on-site literacy coaches and regular support 2 days a month per school. These professional support resources are available throughout the entire length of the project.

The Tier 1 professional development is based on the Strategies for Literacy Independence across the Curriculum model (SLIC) (McDonald, Thornley, Staley, & Moore, 2009). The SLIC curriculum is focused on orienting students to print, using the form and surface features of expository, persuasive text, and narrative texts. Teachers alert students to and question them about the ways in which authors provide information in headings, subheadings, tables, and maps, and how this information can provide the reader with background knowledge of the information to be conveyed in the running text. In narrative text the focus moves into the structure of the plot and the author's use of language and literary features. Students are also taught through scaffolded instruction and independent reading and writing practices strategies for learning vocabulary, notetaking, and analysis of writing prompts.

The SLIC literacy strategies are the same for both Tier 1 and Tier 2 interventions. Students considered eligible are provided dedicated instructional time focused on reading and writing development, with the same literacy strategies delivered by all teachers in the whole-school intervention. In other words, eligible students receive literacy support through Tier l, Tier 2, and their compulsory language arts classes

Student progress is monitored every 8 to 12 weeks, using a common assessment tool designed in cooperation with SLIC developers, San Diego Schools, and UC Berkeley. The assessment system starts from the position that the assessment instrument is always secondary; that prior to developing any item or any method of scoring responses the goals of the curriculum and teachers should be considered first (Wilson, 2005). Therefore, the assessment process is collaborative.

The Striving Readers project assessment is grounded in the principle that it should be embedded in normal classroom activity and based upon authentic instructional tasks. Thus, the progress-monitoring tool is a rubric describing the development of literacy skills as progressing from a foundation of using surface features to navigate and predict the content of unfamiliar text, to a deeper understanding of content within and across texts, to an ability to infer meaning of unfamiliar vocabulary from context, to a critical appreciation of authorial intent and the choices authors make in crafting text.

Sixteen full-length assessments have been developed based on these principles to three types of texts—expository, persuasive, and narrative—across 4 grade levels (7th through 10th). The assessment system includes a pre-test, post-test, and several intermediate benchmark assessments at grades 7, 8, 9, and 10 (sixteen assessments, four per grade level). The goal is for teachers to monitor the progress of their students throughout the year and to allow the tracking of individual students across grade levels. These project assessments were developed, piloted, and designed in partnership with school district leaders and educational researchers and refined based on feedback from teachers and coaches.

The Striving Readers project has yet to produce the kind of results the developers had expected. However, fidelity of classroom intervention SLIC strategies has reached a medium level of implementation at all schools. Additionally, significant effects have been found on high school students for at least one of the outcome assessments, the DRP tests.

Analysis of Case #3

Responsive literacy instruction views adolescents as a resource. There is little evidence that in spite of the cultural diversity of San Diego schools the Striving Readers project is crafting responsive literacy instruction around this diversity. Who we are is integral to the ways we express ourselves. This may be particularly critical for adolescents who are occupied on a near daily basis with identity concerns. Language minority youth entering our secondary schools in ever-increasing numbers often have issues of identity at stake. Although most English learners acquire English language proficiency to one degree or another, many of them have problems with adjustment and identity that may go unaddressed in school. We know that students who bring to school a discourse of home and community that is similar to academic discourse are more likely to experience success (Brozo & Simpson, 2007; Morrell, 2002). For others, however, whose prior knowledge, language, and literacy tools may compete with those of their peers and teachers, achievement and motivation suffer (Moje, Callazo, Carrillo, & Marx, 2001). However, where integration and accommodation of inside- and outside-of-school discourse practices occur, for these students literacy and learning benefits can accrue (Brozo, 2006b; Leander, 2002).

The Striving Readers project would not necessarily have to abandon the SLIC approach to strategic reading and writing to create responsive instruction that attends to youths' backgrounds and competencies. There are numerous ways in which teachers in the project could help youth find connections from the language and knowledge resources they bring to school to the content and concepts under consideration in the classroom. I shared some examples in Chapter 3. At the same time, work on word learning, higher-level comprehension, text structure, and writing could be integrated into practices that honor student diversity.

Responsive literacy instruction occurs within comprehensive literacy programs. There is every indication from the case information on San Diego's Striving Readers project that the architects intended this to be a whole-school initiative. The fact that PD focuses on disciplinary teachers and is ongoing throughout the year and life of the project, makes it clear the responsibility for leavening the literacy competencies of students should not rest solely on the English/language arts teachers' shoulders (Langer, 2002).

To build on these initiatives, project activity for striving readers could be situated within a schoolwide effort to expand reading competence, build independence, and, most significant, increase the desire to read. Programs like Sustained Silent Reading, which have been shown to exert a positive influence on achievement and motivation (Brozo & Hargis, 2003; Fisher, 2004), could enrich the work of classroom teachers with SLIC strategies in the project middle and high schools.

Responsive literacy instruction provides special supports but not always special settings. The Striving Readers project employs a cascading approach in which Tier 2 eligible students receive literacy instruction at three levels: regular language arts class, Tier 1 SLIC strategies in every content classroom, and Tier 2 SLIC targeted interventions in a special reading class. This approach ensures struggling readers receive an intensive level of literacy instruction and are not pulled out of the general education classroom to receive it.

The tiered approach in the San Diego project schools at the middle and high school levels is plagued, nonetheless, by scheduling challenges similar to those experienced in the Lincoln middle schools. Tier 2 students must sacrifice an elective course for one targeting reading specific SLIC interventions. Although this may be the only way to find time in a student's day for focused, systematic instruction, it risks denying a student who may already be disaffected with school the opportunity to experience a pleasurable school experience by exploring a topic of choice. As we have seen, this is no small matter for adolescents, whose choices and independent decision making seem to be expanding everywhere but in school (Heron, 2003; McCarthy & Moje, 2002).

A potentially viable alternative to homogenous grouping of struggling readers in special classes in the San Diego project schools is teaming (Flowers, Mertens, & Mulhall, 1999; Mertens & Flowers, 2004), in which a reading specialist or learning disabilities teacher works side-by-side with a content classroom teacher. Keeping struggling readers in the general education classroom ensures they get exposure to critical content information and ideas while receiving individualized and small-group support from an extra teacher. This approach has at least three potential benefits. First, since a skillful team interacts and supports all students, it tends to limit struggling readers being stigmatized as failing by their peers. Second, it allows the special team teacher to differentiate instruction for each struggling reader within a class (Tomlinson, 2004; 2005; Tomlinson et al., 2004). Third, it can increase a struggling reader's motivation as they are given support in applying strategies directly to text from which they must learn.

Responsive literacy instruction includes more than a curriculum of basic skills redux. The Striving Readers project SLIC strategies would appear to be commensurate with those adolescent readers need for academic success. Learning to take advantage of text structures within specific disciplines, notetaking, and study reading and writing will build struggling readers' competency and agency (Greenleaf & Hinchman, 2009). And the assessments, both for placement and monitoring progress, are appropriate to this goal. The Degrees of Reading Power (DRP), for example, measure paragraph and passage comprehension; and the monitoring tool has been designed to measure specific instructional elements of SLIC along a continuum of competence.

Responsive literacy instruction comes from effective teachers who have the knowledge and practices to address struggling adolescent readers' needs. The level and extent of PD provided in the Striving Readers project is critical to building teacher efficacy in the SLIC strategies. Teachers in the project are sensitized to the reading and writing challenges faced by many of their students and given tools to limit reading and learning failure for struggling readers. Indications are that a majority of teachers are using the SLIC strategies, although student achievement gains have not yet been documented.

Teaching students to use reading and writing strategies may eventually help raise achievement for struggling readers in the San Diego project schools, but there are other student needs the teachers could learn to address. Linked closely to the process of identity construction is what it means for adolescents to be competent and literate learners in both academic and out-of-school contexts. Many adolescents who possess talent, energy, and intelligence find themselves in school settings where these competencies may go untapped (Hinchman, Alvermann, Boyd, Brozo, & Vacca, 2003/2004). The results of failing to align school curricula with students' interests and outside-of-school competencies are not inconsequential. Alvermann and her colleagues (Alvermann, Boyd, Brozo, Hinchman, Moore, & Sturtevant, 2002) assert that:

> our nation's schools have not always recognized and made use of the very real but widely disparate abilities of our nation's adolescents. Their diversity, the result of individual differences and life trajectories, as well as community differences and cultural backgrounds, are too often seen as liabilities rather than as the helpful opportunities for education they can be. In spite of a growing body of scholarship on the intellectual, emotional, and social needs of teenagers, most schools have not employed the curricula and instructional methods this work suggests. (p. 6)

In Chapter 3, I described instructional practices that used adolescents' interests in and competencies with youth media, such as music and computer games, as segues to academic texts and learning. San Diego teachers at the project schools need to be as aware of these youth literacies and how to exploit them in the classroom as they are of SLIC strategies if they want to sustain students' engagement with the strategies, and make learning relevant and more responsive (Alvermann, 2004).

CHAPTER SUMMARY

Working with extant descriptions on websites as well as phone interviews and, in the case of Liberty Middle School, a site visit, I have presented case information about three schools/school systems that have attempted to implement an RTI-like approach in middle and high schools. Although the three settings are very different—rural Virginia, the United States heartland, and urban Southern California—commonalities exist among the ways in which RTI is being applied. The schools in each case use standardized assessments for placement into learning settings described as tiers and marked by different types and levels of intervention. All three use additional measures to gauge student progress within each tier. In this way, the approaches to RTI in these three secondary level cases have much in common with the ways in which RTI has been implemented at the elementary level (McGill-Franzen, Payne, & Dennis, 2010). Moreover, in two of the settings, assessments of foundational reading skills are used, and adolescents who find they qualify for Tier 2 interventions based on these assessments are put into off-the-shelf programs designed to teach basic skills.

In my analysis of these cases from the perspective of the five principles of responsive literacy instruction, I have stressed the importance of secondary RTI-like approaches to make literacy assessment and instruction student centered, comprehensive, engaging, and relevant to the authentic reading and writing needs of adolescents. Furthermore, I have urged that the case schools make room in language and disciplinary curricula for students' different experiences and outside-of-school discourses that are expressed through a variety of media. This means the teachers in these schools who are responsible for providing disciplinary literacy instruction in the classroom or interventions in some other setting need to know more about the funds of knowledge and discourse competencies youth bring with them to middle and secondary school (Jetton & Dole, 2004; Strickland & Alvermann, 2004). Coming to know adolescent students in this way will build on students' strengths for developing academic knowledge and skills (Hull & Schultz, 2002), and lead to more responsive instruction that integrates in- and beyond-school literacy and learning practices (Lee, 1997; Moje et al., 2004; Schultz, 2002).

Relate to Integrate

Whether you are working individually or with a group, take a few moments to reflect on the chapter you have just read. To facilitate your learning, consider the following:

1. **Using the framework of the five principles of Responsive Literacy Instruction, how is your school addressing the literacy needs of all students?**

Individual: Consider your students, who would you view as Tier 1, Tier 2, and Tier 3 level students? Contemplate the ways in which your school is meeting the literacy needs of students. Record your thoughts in a journal reflection.

Group: Display the five principles of Responsive Literacy Instruction. Have the facilitator direct the group to contemplate the ways in which their schools are meeting the literacy needs of students with varying levels of literacy. In a facilitator-led discussion, participants should discuss their items and record these under the appropriate principle. Similar items should be identified and/or combined where possible. As a group, look for unifying themes across the framework.

CHAPTER 5

RTI for Secondary Literacy: Where Do We Go from Here?

BECAUSE APPLICATIONS OF RTI-like approaches for secondary literacy are still so new and sporadic, there is little upon which to base speculation about its future. After an extensive search for RTI at the secondary level, particularly in senior high schools, I have found that only in a limited number of schools and district across the United States is the approach occurring with any vigor. And where it is occurring, architects and advocates are too often trying to fit an elementary-level structure of RTI into the enormously complex world of secondary schools.

LOOKING BACK TO SEE FORWARD

A sign that RTI as implemented in schools thus far has outrun RTI as evidence-based practice is the growing number of dissenters from among the learning and reading disabilities scholarly community (c.f., Kavale, Kauffman, Bachmeir, & LeFever, 2008). Epitomizing this backlash are the criticisms leveled by Reynolds and Shaywitz (2009), who say:

> Response to Intervention (RTI) models of diagnosis and intervention are being implemented rapidly throughout the schools. The purposes of invoking an RTI model for disabilities in the schools clearly are laudable, yet close examination reveals an unappreciated paucity of empirical support for RTI and an overly optimistic view of its practical, problematic issues. Models are being put into practice without adequate research and logistical support and neglect the potential negative long-term impact on students with disabilities. Many implementation problems exist: 1. the vagaries of critical details of the model in practice; 2. the lack of consideration of bright struggling readers; 3. the relativeness, contextual, situation dependent nature of who is identified; 4. the worrisome shortcomings of the RTI process as a means of diagnosis or determination of a disability; and 5. the apparent lack of student-based data to guide effective choice of approaches and components of intervention. (p. 130)

Reynolds and Shaywitz's critique of RTI focuses on students who already possess a learning disabilities label and are receiving services within this approach. Nonetheless, their assertions point to real and potential shortcomings of RTI as a prevention and intervention system for secondary literacy. One of their strongest criticisms centers on Tier 1, or the general education classroom, where they argue teachers are not employing instructional practices that are responsive to reading and learning needs of all students. They conclude by urging systematic monitoring and assessment of intervention fidelity by "independent professionals and not those involved in direct service delivery" (p. 143).

In connection with this last point, evidence of the effectiveness RTI approaches for secondary literacy gathered in systematic ways, especially by outside evaluators, is rare. One exception may be the Texas Adolescent Literacy Academies (TALA). TALA is an approach to RTI for literacy that has been in place in Texas middle schools for the past few years. TALA has been evaluated by a consulting service firm external to the academies. Although indications of improvements in teacher fidelity to the TALA intervention routines and student achievement have been documented, the evaluation has also uncovered aspects of the approach that call into question whether TALA middle schools can sustain the RTI reforms. For instance, in at least some of the schools where the evaluations took place, regular teachers had been replaced by specially trained paraprofessionals and aids to ensure, according to TALA designers, fidelity to the RTI assessment and instructional regimen. This drastic move may achieve the goal of ensuring teacher adherence to the TALA RTI protocol, but is an unrealistic model to export to schools where TALA resources are not present.

The impulse to control who delivers RTI services at the middle school level is a clear reminder of how the complexities of secondary-school teaching and learning culture can confound a vision of RTI formed by those who have a learning disabilities and elementary-level perspective. Stated simply, the reality of RTI for secondary literacy is often much different than advocates envision. This is because attempting to implement RTI with existing secondary-school staff entails a messy and involved process of, among many other things, finding room within the school day for Tiers 2 and 3 activities and accommodating the class scheduling needs of students. Then the hard work really begins, such as convincing Tier 1 teachers of the value of the reforms, requiring disciplinary teachers to become supporters of students' literacy and to differentiate instruction for every student, and providing intensive and ongoing professional development on RTI assessment and instructional practices.

Meanwhile, as learning disabilities scholars and neuroscientists squabble about whether RTI practices are empirically and scientifically based (Fuchs, Mock, Morgan, & Young, 2003; Naglieri, 2007; Shaywitz, 2008), RTI proliferates at the elementary level and will likely grow in use with older students (Goetze, Laster, & Ehren, 2010; Scammacca et al., 2007). Considering the claims by some of its staunchest advocates (Fletcher & Vaughn, 2009; Gresham, Restori, & Cook, 2008; Reschly, 2005), it would seem there is a consensus view of RTI as an empirical model with well-established practices. This is far from the truth (Fuchs & Deshler, 2007; Kavale, Kauffman,

Bachmeir, & LeFever, 2008; Reynolds & Shaywitz, 2009), as I have pointed out in Chapter 1. The gap between rhetoric and reality surrounding RTI has led Reynolds and Shaywitz (2009) to assert:

> Questioning RTI is seen by some as nearly heretical, taking the position that those who oppose immediate, indepth application of the RTI model now are simply uninformed. Like much in special education, RTI is characterized by moral imperative and political activism rather than science. (p. 134)

It seems to me that although these debates and controversies may derive from a sincere desire to explore assessment and instructional options created by IDEA 2004 for learning disability prevention and intervention, they are not enlightening of approaches to secondary literacy that will make a genuine difference in the lives of youth. After all, since the introduction of perhaps the most influential literacy reforms in a lifetime, the NCLB Act, reading and writing achievement for 8th- and 12th-graders as measured by the National Assessment of Educational Progress (NAEP, 2010) has remained flat and is still significantly below the level achieved by these age groups in 1992.

When NCLB was signed into law in 2003, then-President George W. Bush predicted a revolution in reading and the elimination of racial achievement disparities. Instead, after billions were spent and the government's enforcer of the reading revolution, Reading First, was wracked by scandal and discredited by Congress and the courts, U.S. adolescent literacy achievement is no better today than it was then. Racial and gender disparities are as large as they have always been. What is more, compared with peer nations around the globe, American teens barely mustered an average reading literacy achievement score on PISA (Program for International Student Assessment); a score that has been unchanged for nearly a decade (OECD, 2010).

IS RTI FOR SECONDARY LITERACY WORTH SALVAGING?

Given the numerous concerns about RTI, the question is whether it is a promising enough idea for secondary literacy that it should be preserved and improved. Allington (2009a) has offered 10 sensible

(text continues on p. 138)

RTI in the Real World

WESTERN GREENBRIER MIDDLE SCHOOL

Western Greenbrier Middle School (WGMS) is a small, rural school situated in Crawley, West Virginia. This small school serves a population of about 325 6th-, 7th- and 8th-grade students with a nearly homogeneous population of Caucasian students. Approximately 62% of the students attending WGMS receive free or reduced lunches. In past years, the school has experienced declining scores in the core academic areas as measured by state standardized testing. Funding for Tier 3 reading, math, and tutoring/enrichment is provided by a Block 21 grant. Since implementing an RTI process, the school has reported significant gains in reading and mathematics cut scores. Last year WGMS reported the highest gains of all secondary schools in Greenbrier County, West Virginia, with a 9% increase in reading scores and a 12% increase in mathematics scores.

The RTI program at WGMS is a traditional, three-tiered RTI approach, which the principal describes as a re-teach, re-loop, and enrich system. Universal screening data is provided by the WESTEST 2, a summative test of West Virginia's Content Standard Objectives (CSO). The test is given at the end of each school year and tests students across all content areas. Students entering WGMS are placed in the appropriate tiers based on data from 5th-grade testing. West Virginia has adopted the Acuity™ program which is at the heart of the RTI program, and is utilized in all three tiers. The program is aligned with the CSOs and accesses resources from the standards to deliver computer-based instruction that targets instruction in deficient areas. The program also generates formative assessments that are used in the process of progress monitoring.

In order to deliver the appropriate support to all students, teachers are offered professional development opportunities through a summer academy that focuses on teaching instruction and delivery of reading and math strategies. In addition to the summer academy, teachers participate in Professional Learning Communities, which meet monthly and share successful strategies and practices. WGMS has built in a daily 45-minute flex period, which every student attends. During the flex period, every teacher and all instructional support personnel are utilized in order to lessen the student to teacher ratio and to provide additional teaching assistance. Instructional support personnel include a tech specialist, certified reading teachers, and certified math teachers. The flex period instruction varies both by instructional support level and content area.

For each of the academic areas tested, WESTEST 2 categorizes student performance as Novice, Partial Mastery, Mastery, Above Mastery or Distinguished. Students who are categorized as either Novice or Partial Mastery are targeted for Tier 2 or Tier 3 interventions. All others are slated for Tier 1 interventions. Flex period instruction is designed using data from the WESTEST 2 and focuses either on enrichment or remediation-based activities depending on the intervention level. Priority is given to reading and mathematics deficiencies. For students who require Tier 1 support, instruction during the flex period focuses on enrichment activities; for students who require Tier 2 or Tier 3 supports, instruction is based on correcting deficiencies.

Two times during each 9-week grading period, students are given benchmark assessments based on the objectives generated by the Acuity program. A team of teachers and administrators reviews the data in order to determine if the students have achieved proficiency in the deficient area. Students who have sufficiently improved in these areas are then either re-looped to another area of deficiency or moved to a Tier 1 enrichment block.

Western Greenbrier Middle School focuses a great deal of resources on improving reading: each Tier 1 reading classroom is staffed with a certified reading teacher. Each day at the Tier 1 level students attend both a 40-minute block of reading and a 40-minute block of language arts instruction. The reading teacher uses a variety of reading resources that are aimed at improving comprehension, vocabulary, and fluency. The Acuity program is utilized during the classroom period to individualize instruction based on performance on content objectives. Teachers use a variety of formative assessments, such as the San Diego Quick Assessment of Reading Ability, as part of the progress monitoring process. The Scholastic Reading Inventory (SRI) is administered to provide a Lexile measure of student reading ability. This information is also helpful in grouping students for activities, differentiating instruction, and providing a personalized reading list for each student, based on reading ability. The personalized reading list is especially useful in supporting the Sustained Uninterrupted Reading for Fun (SURF) period, which is offered at each tier during the flex block every Friday.

During the flex block, the Tier 1 students attend an enrichment block focused on one of the core content areas. The flex block features a lower teacher to student ratio, with a target maximum of 20 students. Students loop through the different content areas throughout the course of the year. During the reading/language arts flex block, students are offered both group and individualized instruction that is intended to augment and enrich the instruction given in the Tier 1 classrooms. Again, the Acuity program is used to generate reading resources and activities that are based on the student's performance on the content standards objectives.

For Tier 2 students, the flex block also has a lower student to teacher ratio, with a target of 10 students and a maximum of 15 students. For Tier 2 instruction, students are grouped by skill deficiencies based on CSOs. Both language arts teachers and certified reading teachers are utilized in the Tier 2 reading classroom. Many of the same strategies that are used at the Tier 1 level are used at the Tier 2 level, but with more individualized instruction and closer progress monitoring. In addition to these, the Lindamood Phoneme Sequencing program (LiPS) and Wilson Reading System are also used. The Acuity program is used to generate reading resources and computer-based activities that are based on the student's performance on the content standards objectives. Students are kept in the Tier 2 supports until mastery is achieved. Once achieved, students are moved to the enrichment block where more challenging, critical thinking skills are offered

Students who are not making adequate gains with the Tier 1 and Tier 2 supports are recommended for Tier 3 interventions. Tier 3 students are offered both the Tier 1 and Tier 2 supports, but in addition receive Tier 3 support in an after-school tutoring program. Tutoring is offered 3 days per week for 1½ hours, during which students are given individualized instruction. For students with reading deficiencies, Lindamood Phoneme Sequencing program (LiPS) and Wilson Reading System are also used in addition to Acuity program.

CRITICAL QUESTIONS:

- Western Greenbrier Middle School puts students who qualify for Tier 2 into programs that focus on foundational reading skills, such as phonics and phonemic awareness. What alternatives to these program approaches could you recommend for helping adolescents increase basic reading competencies?
- Western Greenbrier Middle instituted a 45-minute flex period to ensure every teacher is available to provide extra reading and learning support to students. Is this option feasible in your own school? What other options might be possible for an entire school staff to offer daily extra support to students?
- Sustained Uninterrupted Reading for Fun (SURF) time is Western Greenbrier's approach to promoting recreational reading. What are your experiences with sustained silent reading programs? How else can middle school students be motivated to read for enjoyment?

recommendations for salvaging RTI at the primary and elementary levels. Here are my five recommendations for the literacy development of youth at the secondary level.

1. Don't allow RTI to define the secondary school reading program. Instead, middle and high schools should be identified by their comprehensiveness and responsiveness. As we have seen, RTI is linked far too closely to learning disabilities and special education to be a viable approach for an overall secondary literacy program. This is because literacy for adolescents involves so much more than remedial reading and writing (Alvermann, 2003; Brozo & Simpson, 2007; Sturtevant et al., 2006). The developmental and domain-specific nature of literacy necessitates a program with features designed to address the academic literacy needs of all students, regardless of label. A comprehensive approach to adolescent literacy should also take into account that literacy achievement is tied closely to motivation and identity concerns of youth. Finally, to be truly responsive a secondary literacy program should honor youth literacies and new media.

A comprehensive program to adolescent literacy can be built on the recommendations of countless valuable reports for reforming adolescent literacy (e.g., *Reading Next* by Biancarosa and Snow, 2004), which provide guidelines and goals for reform without specifying the practices for meeting the goals. Specific instructional practices should be determined by the teachers and teacher leaders in each district and school.

2. Don't fixate on foundational reading skills for adolescents. If RTI at the secondary level is organized and delivered by special education personnel, like it so often is at the elementary level, then instructional approaches that focus on basic reading skills will likely dominate. This is the case in spite of the fact that IDEA does not even provide roles for special educators in RTI. Nonetheless, most schools' direct funding for RTI is through special education (Allington, 2009a).

I have made the case plain that adolescents need much more than basic skills. For all the reasons outlined in this book, adolescent literacy requires attention to reading comprehension and more complex thinking skills, even for struggling readers (Stroud & Reynolds, 2009). Indeed, evidence from students in RTI systems suggests they do best when comprehension strategies are taught along with basic skills (Stroud & Reynolds, 2009).

Instead of focusing on basic reading skills, approaches to secondary literacy should concentrate on essential study reading and writing strategies that are needed by youth in order to profit from complex texts and have overall academic success (Ehren & Deshler, 2009; Graham & Perin, 2007; Heller & Greenleaf, 2007).

3. Don't become paralyzed by evidence-based practice if it isn't working. *Evidence* is a value-laden word. What looks like evidence in support of certain literacy practices to some may be unconvincing to others (Krashen, 2008). I agree with Reynolds and Shaywitz (2009), who in spite of their neuroscience orientation, acknowledge that they "recognize the need for differentiated instruction driven by student characteristics and do not subscribe to the 'one instructional model . . . fits all'" (p. 140). To accept that no single set of instructional strategies, programs, or assessments will be adequate opens the way for an approach that is truly responsive to youths' reading and learning needs. Such an approach must be flexible and "driven by student characteristics," not by a rigid assessment and instructional protocol applied to all (McEneaney, Lose, & Schwartz, 2006).

When the R of RTI becomes *responsive* instead of *response*, a critical shift occurs away from evaluating a student's responses to fixed and predetermined methods to evaluating the responsiveness of the methods themselves. In this way, practices and strategies will undergo constant scrutiny as to how responsive they are to an individual student's reading and learning needs. Based on this continual evaluation, students will be offered customized literacy instruction focused on their evolving interests and learning requirements.

Instead of relying on off-the-shelf packages and licensed instructional regimens, secondary teachers should focus on the literacy and learning goals for individual students and provide responsive practices that meet those goals. Secondary teachers should also engage in collaborative action research (Gordon, 2008) as a way of gathering context-specific information about the effectiveness of their literacy practices and approaches, and introduce appropriate instructional modifications as a result (Goswami, Lewis, Rutherford, & Waff, 2009; Lankshear & Knobel, 2004).

4. Honor youth literacies. Conspicuously absent from RTI schemes is any acknowledgment of the importance of youth literacies to their identities as adolescents and learners. Secondary schools that honor the literacies and discourses of youth realize that they and all of us live in what O'Brien (2001) calls the *mediasphere*. I describe the mediasphere as "a world saturated by inescapable, ever-evolving, and competing media that both flow through us and are altered and created by us" (Brozo, 2005, p. 534). Adolescents are the most active participants in the mediasphere, creating forms of discourse that should be acknowledged and appreciated in school settings, since competency in these new forms of communication will serve youth well in the ever-evolving global reach of the digital age (Lankshear & Knobel, 2002). Secondary school is the setting where youths' multiple literacies could find expression in the understanding, critical analysis, and reinterpretation of concepts and content (Guzzetti, Elliott, & Welsch, 2010; Hagood, Alvermann, & Heron-Hruby, 2010).

Coming to terms with what counts as literacy in youths' lives and in the worlds they inhabit is a challenge for special and general education teachers alike. However, it is essential that secondary teachers create room in the curriculum for students' out-of-school competencies with new literacies and media in order to build on students' strengths for developing academic knowledge and skills (Hinchman et al., 2003/2004; Hull & Schultz, 2002; Morrell, 2002). An instructive example of the power of bringing adolescents and new media together comes from Goodman (2003), who found by helping a group of struggling high school students in New York City create their own documentary about gun violence in their neighborhoods, he could expand the teens' literacy and thinking skills while building confidence in learning.

It's clear that those responsible for the literacy development of secondary students need to know more about the funds of knowledge and discourse competencies they bring with them to middle and high school classrooms (Jetton & Dole, 2004; Strickland & Alvermann, 2004). Coming to know students in this way will lead to more responsive instruction that integrates in- and beyond-school literacy and learning practices (Lee, 1997; Moje et al., 2004; Schultz, 2002).

5. Channel resources into pd for general education disciplinary teachers so that prevention gets the lion's share of attention. Our secondary school classrooms are more diverse now than at any time in the history of U.S. schooling (National Center for Education Statistics, 2010; National Clearinghouse for English Language Acquisition, 2010). This diversity presents advocates of secondary literacy programs with considerable challenges (Kungner & Edwards, 2006). One such challenge is crafting responsive instruction in the content classroom to ensure all youth develop literacy and learning skills to acquire information and concepts in the content areas (Brozo & Puckett, 2009).

Pressure on classroom teachers to integrate literacy instruction into their disciplinary lessons is coming from the Common Core State Standards Initiative (CCSSI; www.corestandards.org). Common core proponents want to see a shift in prevailing literacy curriculum from a focus on developing basic reading skills and building fluency toward reading and writing to gain knowledge and express new understandings with informational text (Shanahan & Shanahan, 2008). Reading to build knowledge is critical for English learners and struggling students, if they are to progress adequately through middle and high school (Wassell, Hawrylak, & LaVan, 2010).

Even the title of the common core English language arts standards for grades 6 through 12 makes clear this significant shift in emphasis: "Common Core State Standards for English Language Arts & Literacy in History/Social Studies, Science, and Technical Subjects" (CCSSI, 2010). This new focus on literacy in the service of content learning is defended on the grounds that building "a foundation of knowledge in these fields [will give students] the background to be better readers in all content areas" (CCSSI, 2010, p. 10).

Secondary classroom teachers will need comprehensive and ongoing professional development that guides them in ways to differentiate content literacy instruction for students with diverse abilities and backgrounds (Edyburn, 2003; Fisher & Frey, 2001; Tomlison, 2005). This is an indispensable skill for a classroom teacher working in an RTI program because of the expectation that responsive instruction at Tier 1 will diminish the need for Tiers 2 and 3 supports for most students (Brozo, 2010a).

CHAPTER SUMMARY

Creating a system of literacy supports and enrichment experiences for adolescents in middle and high school has been urged by professionals for many years (Mraz, Rickelman, & Vacca, 2009). All too often, however, adolescent literacy is ignored, marginalized, or de-emphasized in practice and policy in the United States (Vacca, 1998). When it does receive attention, for instance as a result of the recent availability of large federal grant funds, the vision of what comprehensive and responsive adolescent literacy could be is co-opted by those with narrower and, at times, self-serving interests (Santa, 2006).

Unfortunately, while RTI has helped to draw attention to the needs of students beyond the elementary grades, because of its roots in behaviorism and special education, it has also constricted the scope of possibilities for adolescent literacy practices. Proponents insist that RTI interventions must be "scientifically" sound or students will not show improvements. According to this logic, if students fail to show progress, the problem isn't with the interventions

(Kavale, Kauffman, Bachmeier, & LeFever, 2008). In accepting only their "evidence" RTI purists ignore valid but contravening research findings and dismiss instructional options that have potential for success (Allington, 2009a). For secondary teachers working with youth who bring to their classrooms unparalleled diversity, limiting instructional options would seem counterintuitive.

My five recommendations for responsive adolescent literacy derive from the deep understanding that to be a successful reader at the secondary level adolescents need much more than skill in decoding words or the ability to read smoothly and quickly. They must also be knowledgeable of and have control over a range of sophisticated literacy strategies. They need their interests and experiences aligned with school curricula. Instead of reducing the parameters of what counts as literacy to a few basic, core reading skills and strategies, adolescents need learning environments that honor their outside-of-school competencies and discourses expressed through a variety of media. Adolescents need knowledgeable and skillful classroom teachers who can offer responsive literacy instruction to benefit every student and differentiate assistance for those in need of extra support. Finally, secondary students need immersion in a school culture that places a premium on literacy through a comprehensive array of related and supportive services.

(This chapter's "Relate to Integrate" section appears on the next page.)

Relate to Integrate

Whether you are working individually or with a group of others, take a few moments to reflect on the chapter which you have just read. To facilitate your learning, consider the following:

1. **The first recommendation for creating a program for secondary literacy that is responsive to all students needs is to avoid making RTI the centerpiece.**

Individual: List the elements of a comprehensive literacy program for a middle school or high school that include features of RTI as one aspect of the program. What other key elements of such a program should be included? Try creating a diagram that shows the relationships among the elements of a comprehensive literacy program you identified.

Group: As a group, discuss the different roles each member should play in a comprehensive secondary literacy program. How can your roles be coordinated to ensure responsive literacy services are provided each student? What obstacles are there to such a program and how might they be overcome? Facilitator will lead discussion.

2. **RTI purists assert that a secondary literacy program must be designed and implemented on the basis of scientific evidence. This strict interpretation of "evidence" may inhibit teachers from exercising sound professional judgment in responding to the day-to-day needs of struggling readers. What counts as evidence in your teaching context?**

Individual: Read about teacher action research from available online and/or university library resources. Implement a responsive literacy strategy of your own design. Gather and analyze evidence of the effect on a struggling reader. If your practices are effective, how could you present a persuasive case for teacher research data as valid evidence?

Group: Together, plan a collaborative action research project around a literacy practice or issue. Delineate roles, methods, data-gathering and data-analysis tools. Meet periodically to update progress. Analyze the data and establish results. Share the results with administration and colleagues and discuss how they can be used to guide school practices and policy.

References

ACT. (2005). *Average national ACT score unchanged in 2005: Students graduate from high school ready or not.* Retrieved June 11, 2009, from http://www.act.org/news/releases/2005/8-17-05.html

Alger, C. (2007). Engaging student teachers' hearts and minds in the struggle to address (il)literacy in content area classrooms. *Journal of Adolescent and Adult Literacy, 50*(8), 620–630.

Allington, R. L. (2002). What I've learned about effective reading instruction. *Phi Delta Kappan, 83*(10), 740–747.

Allington, R. L. (2008). *What really matters in Response to Intervention: Research-based designs.* Boston: Allyn & Bacon.

Allington, R. L. (2009a). RTI: Ten principles for saving a promising idea. *The Literacy Professional, 19*(2), 2.

Allington, R. L. (2009b). *What really matters in fluency.* New York: Pearson.

Allington, R. L., & McGill-Franzen, A. (1989a). Different programs, indifferent instruction. In A. Gartner & D. Lipsky (Eds.), *Beyond separate education: Quality education for all* (pp. 75–98). Baltimore: Brookes.

Allington, R. L., & McGill-Franzen, A. (1989b). School response to reading failure: Chapter 1 and special education students in grades 2, 4, & 8. *Elementary School Journal, 89*(5), 529–542.

Allington, R. L., McGill-Franzen, A., Camilli, G., Williams, L., Graff, J., Zeig, J., Zmach, C., & Nowak, R. (2010). Addressing summer reading setback among economically disadvantaged elementary students. *Reading Psychology, 31*(5), 411–427.

Allington, R. L., & Walmsley, S. A. (2007). *No quick fix: Rethinking literacy programs in America's elementary schools* [The RTI edition]. New York: Teachers College Press.

Alvermann, D. E. (2002). Effective literacy instruction for adolescents. *Journal of Literacy Research, 34*(2), 189–208.

Alvermann, D. E. (2003). *Seeing themselves as capable and engaged readers: Adolescents and re/mediated instruction.* Naperville, IL: Learning Point Associates. Retrieved February 9, 2011, from http://www.learningpt.org/pdfs/literacy/readers.pdf

Alvermann, D. E. (Ed.). (2004). *Adolescents and literacies in a digital world.* New York: Peter Lang.

Alvermann, D. E., Boyd, F., Brozo, W., Hinchman, K., Moore, D., & Sturtevant, E. (2002). *Principled practices for a literate America: A framework for literacy and learning in the upper grades.* New York: Carnegie Corporation.

Alvermann, D. E., & Moore, D. W. (1991). Secondary school reading. In R. Barr, M. L. Kamil, P. B. Mosenthal, & P. D. Pearson (Eds.), *Handbook of reading research* (Vol. 2, pp. 951–983). White Plains, NY: Longman.

Alvermann, D. E., & Rush, L. S. (2004). Literacy intervention programs at the middle and high school levels. In T. L. Jetton & J. A. Dole (Eds.), *Adolescent literacy research and practice* (pp. 210–227). New York: Guilford.

Anderman, E. M., Maehr, M. L., & Midgley, C. (1999). Declining motivation after the transition to middle school: Schools can make a difference. *Journal of Research and Development in Education, 32*(3), 131–147.

Anders, P. (2002). Secondary reading programs: A story of what was. In D. Schallert, C. Fairbanks, J. Worthy, B. Maloch, & J. Hoffman (Eds.), *51st Yearbook of the National Reading Conference* (pp. 82–93). Oak Creek, WI: National Reading Conference.

Applebaum, M. (2009). *The one-stop guide to implementing RTI: Academic and behavioral interventions, K–12*. Thousand Oaks, CA: Corwin.

Archer, A. L., Gleason, M. M., & Vachon, V. L. (2003). Decoding and fluency: Foundation skills for struggling older readers. *Learning Disabilities Quarterly, 26*(2), 89–102.

Baer, D. M., Wolf, M. M., & Risley, T. R. (1968). Some current dimensions of applied behavior analyses. *Journal of Applied Behavior Analysis, 1*(1), 91–97.

Barnett, D. W., Daly, E. J., Jones, K. M., & Lentz, F. E. (2004). Response to intervention: Empirically based special service decisions from single-case designs of increasing and decreasing intensity. *Journal of Special Education, 38*(2), 66–79.

Batsche, G. M. (2005, October). *Implementing the problem-solving/response to intervention protocols: Implications for school social workers*. Paper presented at the annual conference of Florida Association of School Social Workers, Jacksonville, FL.

Batsche, G., Elliot, J., Graden, J. L., Grimes, J., Kovaleski, J. F., Prasse, D., Reschly, D. J., Schrag, J., & Tilly, W. D., III. (2005). *Response to intervention: Policy considerations and implementation*. Alexandria, VA: National Association of State Directors of Special Education.

Beers, K. (1996). No time, no interest, no way: The three voices of aliteracy. *School Library Journal, 42*(2), 30–41.

Beers, K. (2003). *When kids can't read: What teachers can do*. Portsmouth, NH: Heinemann.

Beers, K., Probst, R., & Rief, L. (2007). *Adolescent literacy: Turning promise into practice*. Portsmouth, NH: Heinemann.

Belfanz, R. (2009). Can the American high school become an avenue of advancement for all? *The Future of Children, 19*(1), 17–36.

Bender, W. N., & Shores, C. (2007). *Response to intervention: A practical guide for every teacher*. Thousand Oaks, CA: Corwin.

Bender, W. N., Ulmer, L., Baskette, M. R., & Shores, C. (2007). Will RTI work? Ongoing questions. In W. N. Bender & C. Shores (Eds.), *Response to intervention: A practice guide for every teacher* (pp. 91–110). Thousand Oaks, CA: Corwin.

Best, R., Rowe, M., Ozuru, Y., McNamara, D. (2005). Deep-level comprehension of science texts: The role of the reader and the text. *Topics in Language Disorders, 25*(1), 65–83.

Bhattacharya, A., & Ehri, L. C. (2004). Graphoysyllabic analysis helps adolescent struggling readers read and spell words. *Journal of Learning Disabilities, 37*(4), 331–349.

Biancarosa, G., & Snow, C. (2004). *Reading next: A vision for action and research in middle and high school literacy*. New York/Washington, DC: Carnegie Corporation/Alliance for Excellent Education. Retrieved February 10, 2005, from www.all4ed.org

Blevins, W. (2001). *Teaching phonics and word study in the intermediate grades*. New York: Scholastic.

Bloome, D., & Green, J. (1984). Directions in the sociolinguistic study of reading. In P. D. Pearson (Ed.), *Handbook of reading research* (pp. 395–421). New York: Longman.

Board on Children, Youth, and Families. (2003). *Engaging schools: Fostering high school students' motivation to learn*. Washington, DC: National Academies Press.

Bomer, R. (1999). Conferring with struggling readers: The test of our craft, courage, and hope. *The New Advocate, 12*(1), 21–38.

Bradley, R., Danielson, L., & Doolittle, J. (2007). Responsiveness to Intervention: 1997 to 2007. *Teaching Exceptional Children, 39*(5), 8–12.

Braunger, J., Donahue, D., Evans, K., & Galguera, T. (2005). *Rethinking preparation for content area teaching*. San Francisco: Jossey Bass.

Brown-Chidsey, R., & Steege, M. W. (2005). *Response to intervention: Principles and strategies for effective practice*. New York: Guilford.

Brozo, W. G. (1990). Learning how at-risk readers learn best: A case for interactive assessment. *Journal of Reading, 33*(1), 522–527.

Brozo, W. G. (1995). Literacy without "risk": Reconsidering cultural and curricular differentiation in literacy. *State of Reading, 2*(2), 5–12.

Brozo, W. G. (2005). Book review: Adolescents and literacies in a digital world. *Journal of Literacy Research, 36*(4), 533–538.

Brozo, W. G. (2006a). Tales out of school: Accounting for adolescents in a literacy reform community. *Journal of Adolescent & Adult Literacy, 49*(5), 410–418.

Brozo, W. G. (2006b). Authentic contexts for developing language tools in vocational education. In J. Flood, D. Lapp, & N. Farnan (Eds.), *Content area reading and learning: Instructional strategies* (pp. 349–361). Mahwah, NJ: Erlbaum.

Brozo, W. G. (2009/2010). Response to intervention or responsive instruction? Challenges and possibilities of RTI for adolescent literacy. *Journal of Adolescent & Adult Literacy, 53*(4), 277–281.

Brozo, W. G. (2010a). Response to Intervention or responsive instruction? Challenges and possibilities of Response to Intervention for adolescent literacy. *Journal of Adolescent & Adult Literacy, 54*(4), 277–281.

Brozo, W. G. (2010b). The role of content literacy in an effective RTI program. *The Reading Teacher, 64*(2), 147–150.

Brozo, W. G., & Afflerbach, P. P. (2011). *The adolescent literacy inventory: Grades 6–12.* Boston: Pearson.

Brozo, W. G., & Brozo, C. L. (1994). Literacy assessment in standardized and zero-failure contexts. *Reading and Writing Quarterly, 10*(3), 189–208.

Brozo, W. G., & Fisher, D. (2010). Literacy starts with the teachers. *Educational Leadership, 67*(6), 74–77.

Brozo, W. G., & Hargis, C. H. (2003). Taking seriously the idea of reform: One high school's efforts to make reading more responsive to all students. *Journal of Adolescent and Adult Literacy, 47*(1), 14–23.

Brozo, W. G., & Puckett, K. S. (2009). *Supporting content area literacy with technology.* Boston: Allyn & Bacon.

Brozo, W. G., Shiel, G., & Topping, K. (2007/2008). Engagement in reading: Lessons learned from three PISA countries. *Journal of Adolescent & Adult Literacy, 51*(4), 304–315.

Brozo, W. G., & Simpson, M. L. (2007). *Content literacy for today's adolescents: Honoring diversity and building competence.* Upper Saddle River, NJ: Pearson.

Calhoon, M. B., & Fuchs, L. S. (2003). The effects of peer-assisted learning strategies and curriculum-based measurement on the mathematics performance of secondary students with disabilities. *Remedial and Special Education, 24*(4), 235–245.

Cantrell, S. C., Burns, L., & Callaway, P. (2009). Middle- and high-school content area teachers' perceptions about literacy teaching and learning. *Literacy Research and Instruction, 48*(1), 76–94.

Cantrell, S. C., & Hughes, H. K. (2008). Teacher efficacy and content literacy implementation: An exploration of the effects of extended professional development with coaching. *Journal of Literacy Research, 40*(1), 95–127.

Cappella, E., & Weinstein, R. (2001). Turning around reading achievement: Predictors of high school students' academic resilience. *Journal of Educational Psychology, 91*(4), 758–771.

Cassidy, J., & Cassidy, D. (2009). What's hot, what's not for 2009. *Reading Today, 26*(4), 1, 8–9.

Cioffi, G., & Carney, J. J. (1983). Dynamic assessment of reading disability. *The Reading Teacher, 36*(8), 764–768.

Cipielewski, J., & Stanovich, K. (1992). Predicting growth in reading ability from children's exposure to print. *Journal of Experimental Child Psychology, 54*(1), 74–89.

Cobb, B., Sample, P., Alwell, M., & Johns, N. (2005). *The effects of cognitive-behavioral interventions on dropout prevention for youth with disabilities.* Clemson, SC: National Dropout Prevention Center for Students with Disabilities.

Coburn, C. E. (2001). Collective sensemaking about reading: How teachers mediate reading policy in their professional communities. *Educational Evaluation and Policy Analysis, 23*(2), 145–170.

Common Core State Standards Initiative. (2010). *Common Core state standards for English language arts & literacy in history/social studies, science, and technical subjects.* Retrieved June 9, 2010, from www.corestandards.org/assets/CCSSI_ELA%20Standards.pdf

Conley, M. W., & Hinchman, K. A. (2004). No Child Left Behind: What it means for U.S. adolescents and what we can do about it. *Journal of Adolescent & Adult Literacy, 48*(1), 42–50.

Cook-Sather, A. (2002a). Authorizing students' perspectives: Toward trust, dialogue, and change in education. *Educational Researcher, 31*(4), 3–14.

Cook-Sather, A. (2002b, Fall). Re(in)forming the conversations: Student position, power, and voice in teacher education. *Radical Teacher, 64,* 21–28.

Cook-Sather, A. (2002c). A teacher should be . . . When the answer is the question. *Knowledge Quest, 30*(5), 12–15.

Cook-Sather, A. (2003). Listening to students about learning differences. *Teaching Exceptional Children, 35*(4), 22–26.

Cooter, R. B. (2004). *Perspectives on rescuing urban literacy education: Spies, saboteurs, and saints.* Mahwah, NJ: Erlbaum.

Corbett, H. D., & Wilson, R. L. (1995). Make a difference with, not for, students: A plea for researchers and reformers. *Educational Researcher, 24*(5), 12–17.

Cortiella, C. (2005). *A parent's guide to response-to-intervention* [Parent Advocacy Brief]. New York: National Center for Learning Disabilities. Retrieved February 20, 2009, from http://www.ncld.org/images/stories/downloads/parent_center/rti_final.pdf

Dale, E., & O'Roarke, J. (1981). *The living word vocabulary.* Chicago: World Book–Childcraft International.

Daly, E. J., Martens, B. K., Barnet, D., Witt, J. C., & Olson, S. C. (2007). Varying intervention delivery in response to intervention: Confronting and resolving challenges with measurement, instruction, and intensity. *School Psychology Review, 36*(4), 562–581.

Deno, S. L. (1986). Formative evaluation of individual student programs: A new role for school psychologists. *School Psychology Review, 15*(3), 358–374.

Deshler, D. D., Palincsar, A. S., Biancarosa, G., & Nair, M. (2007). *Informed choices for struggling adolescent readers.* Newark, DE: International Reading Association.

Deshler, R. T., Deshler, D. D., & Biancarosa, G. (2007). School and district change to improve adolescent literacy. In D. D. Deshler, A. S. Palincsar, G. Biancarosa, & M. Nair (Eds.), *Informed choices for struggling adolescent readers* (pp. 92–105). Newark, DE: International Reading Association.

Donahue, D. (2003). Reading across the great divide: English and math teachers apprentice one another as readers and disciplinary insiders. *Journal of Adolescent & Adult Literacy, 47*(1), 24–37.

Donahue, P., Daane, M., & Grigg, W. (2003). *The nation's report card: Reading highlights 2003.* Washington, DC: National Center for Education Statistics.

Dong, Y. R. (2002). Integrating language and content: How three biology teachers work with non-English speaking students. *International Journal of Bilingual Education and Bilingualism, 5*(1), 40–57.

Dozier, C. (2006). *Responsive literacy coaching: Tools for creating and sustaining purposeful change.* Portland, ME: Stenhouse.

Draper, R. J. (2008). Redefining content-area literacy teacher education: Finding my voice through collaboration. *Harvard Educational Review, 78*(1), 60–83.

Draper, R. J., Smith, L. K., Hall, K. M., & Sieber, D. (2005). What's more important—literacy or content? Confronting the literacy-content dualism. *Action in Teacher Education, 27*(2), 12–21.

DuBay, W. (2004). *The principles of readability.* Costa Mesa, CA: Impact Education.

Dudley, A. M. (2005, Spring). Rethinking reading fluency for struggling adolescent readers. *Beyond Behavior, 14*(3), 16–22.

Duffy, H. (n.d.). *Meeting the needs of significantly struggling learners in high school: A look at approaches to tiered intervention.* Washington, DC: American Institutes for Research. Retrieved March 15, 2009, from www.betterhighschools.org/docs/NHSC_RTIBrief_08-02-07.pdf

Eccles, J. S., Lord, S., & Buchanan, C. M. (1996). School transitions in early adolescence: What are we doing to our young children? In J. A. Graber, J. Brooks-Gunn, & A. C. Peterson (Eds.), *Transitions through adolescence: Interpersonal domains and context* (pp. 251–284). Hillsdale, NJ: Erlbaum.

Edyburn, D. (2003). Reading difficulties in the general education classroom: A taxonomy of text modification strategies. *Closing the Gap, 21*(6), 1, 10–13, 30–31.

Ehren, B. J., & Deshler, D. D. (2009). *Using the content literacy continuum as a framework for implementing RTI in secondary schools.*

Lawrence: University of Kansas Center for Research on Learning.

Ehri, L., Nuves, S., Stahl, S., & Willows, D. (2001). Systematic phonics instruction helps students to read: Evidence from the National Reading Panel's meta-analysis. *Review of Educational Research, 71*(3), 393–447.

Erikson, E. (1980). *Identity and the life cycle.* New York: W.W. Norton.

Espin, C. A., Busch, T. W., Shin, J., & Kruschwitz, R. (2001). Curriculum-based measurement in the content areas: Validity of vocabulary-matching as an indicator of performance in social studies. *Learning Disabilities Research & Practice, 16*(3), 142–151.

Espin, C. A., & Foegen, A. (1996). Validity of general outcome measures for predicting secondary students' performance on content-area tasks. *Exceptional Children, 62*(6), 497–510.

Fisher, D. (2001). Cross age tutoring: Alternatives to the reading resource room for struggling adolescent readers. *Journal of Instructional Psychology, 28*(4), 234–240.

Fisher, D. (2004). Setting the "opportunity to read" standard: Resuscitating the SSR program in an urban high school. *Journal of Adolescent & Adult Literacy, 48*(2), 138–150.

Fisher, D., Brozo, W. G., Frey, N., & Ivey, G. (2011). *50 instructional routines to develop content literacy.* Upper Saddle River, NJ: Merrill/Prentice Hall.

Fisher, D., & Frey, N. (2001). Access to the core curriculum: Critical ingredients for success. *Remedial and Special Education, 22*(3), 148–157.

Fisher, D., & Ivey, G. (2005). Literacy and language as learning in content area classes: A departure from "every teacher a teacher of reading." *Action in Teacher Education, 27*(2), 3–11.

Fisher, D., & Ivey, G. (2006). Evaluating the interventions for struggling adolescent readers. *Journal of Adolescent and Adult Literacy, 50*(3), 180–189.

Fisher, J., Schumaker, J., & Deshler, D. (2002). Improving the reading comprehension of at-risk adolescents. In C. C. Block & M. Pressley (Eds.), *Comprehension instruction: Research-based best practices* (pp. 351–364). New York: Guilford.

Flanigan, K., & Greenwood, S. C. (2007). Effective content vocabulary instruction in the middle: Matching students, purposes, words, and strategies. *Journal of Adolescent and Adult Literacy, 51*(3), 226–238.

Fletcher, J. M., Coulter, W. A., Reschly, D. J., & Vaughn, S. (2004). Alternative approaches to the definition and identification of learning disabilities: Some questions and answers. *Annals of Dyslexia, 54*(2), 304–331.

Fletcher, J., & Vaughn, S. (2009). Response to intervention: Preventing and remediating academic difficulties. *Child Development Perspectives, 3*(1), 30–37.

Florida Center for Reading Research. (2006). *Intervention and remedial programs for students above third grade.* Tallahassee: Author. Retrieved October 11, 2010, from http://www.fcrr.org/FCRRReports/CReports.aspx?rep=412

Flowers, N., Mertens, S. B., & Mulhall, P. F. (1999). The impact of teaming: Five research-based outcomes. *Middle School Journal, 31*(2), 57–60.

Flynt, S., & Brozo, W. G. (2009). It's all about the teacher. *The Reading Teacher, 62*(6), 536–538.

Foorman, B. R., Francis, D. J., Fletcher, J. M., Schatschneider, C., & Mehta, P. (1998). The role of instruction in learning to read: Preventing reading disabilities in at-risk children. *Journal of Educational Psychology, 90*(1), 37–55.

Foorman, B. R., & Torgesen, J. K. (2001). Critical elements of classroom and small-group instruction promote reading success in all children. *Learning Disabilities Research and Practice, 16*(4), 202–211.

Fuchs, D., & Deshler, D. D. (2007). What we need to know about responsiveness to intervention (and shouldn't be afraid to ask). *Learning Disabilities Research and Practice, 22*(2), 129–136.

Fuchs, D., & Fuchs, L. (2005). Responsiveness-to-intervention: A blueprint for practitioners, policymakers, and parents. *Teaching Exceptional Children, 38*(1), 57–61.

Fuchs, D., & Fuchs, L. (2006). Introduction to Response to Intervention: What, why, and how valid is it? *Reading Research Quarterly, 41*(1), 93–98.

Fuchs, D., Mock, D., Morgan, P. L., & Young, C. L. (2003). Responsiveness-to-intervention: Definitions, evidence, and implications for the learning disabilities construct. *Learning Disabilities Research and Practice, 18*(3), 157–171.

Fuchs, L. S., & Fuchs, D. (2007). The role of assessment in the three-tier approach to reading instruction. In E. Haager, J. Klingner, & S. Vaughn (Eds.), *Evidence-based reading practices for response to intervention* (pp. 29–42). Baltimore, MD: Brookes.

Fullan, M. (2007). *The new meaning of educational change* (4th ed.). New York: Teachers College Press.

Gardiner, S. (2001). Ten minutes a day for silent reading. *Educational Leadership, 59*(2), 32–35.

Gee, J. P. (2000). Discourse and sociocultural studies in reading. In M. Kamil, P. Mosenthal, P. D. Pearson, & R. Barr (Eds.), *Handbook of reading research* (Vol. III, pp. 195–208). Mahwah, NJ: Erlbaum.

Gee, J. P. (2001). Reading as situated language: A sociocognitive perspective. *Journal of Adolescent and Adult Literacy, 44*(8), 714–725.

Gelzheiser, L. M., Scanlon, D. M., & Hallgren-Flynn, L. (2010). Spotlight on RTI for adolescents: An example of intensive middle school intervention using the interactive strategies approach-extended. In M. Y. Lipson & K. K. Wixson (Eds.), *Successful approaches to RTI: Collaborative practices for improving K–12 literacy.* Newark, DE: International Reading Association.

Gersten, R., Compton, D., Connor, C. M., Dimino, J., Santoro, L., Linan-Tompson, S., & Tilly, W. D. (2008). Assisting students struggling with reading: Response to Intervention and multi-tier intervention for reading in the primary grades: A practice guide [NCEE 2009-4045]. Washington, DC: National Center for Education Evaluation and Regional Assistance, Institute of Education Sciences, U.S. Department of Education. Retrieved September 19, 2010, from http://ies.ed.gov/ncee/wwc/publications/practiceguides/

Gersten, R., & Dimino, J. A. (2006). RTI (Response to Intervention): Rethinking special education for students with reading difficulties (yet again). *Reading Research Quarterly, 41*(1), 99–108.

Gillet, J. W., Temple, C., & Crawford, A. N. (2008). *Understanding reading problems: Assessment and instruction* (7th ed.). Boston: Allyn & Bacon.

Goetze, S. K., Laster, B., & Ehren, B. J. (2010). RTI for secondary school literacy. In M. Y. Lipson & K. K. Wixson (Eds.), *Successful approaches to RTI: Collaborative practices for improving K–12 literacy* (pp. 173–210). Newark, DE: International Reading Association.

Goodman, K. (2006). *The truth about DIBELS: What it is—What it does.* Portsmouth, NH: Heinemann.

Goodman, L. (2001). A tool for learning: Vocabulary self-awareness. In C. Blanchfield (Ed.), *Creative vocabulary: Strategies for teaching vocabulary in grades K–12* (pp. 54–63). Fresno, CA: San Joaquin Valley Writing Project.

Goodman, S. (2003). *Teaching youth media: A critical guide to literacy, video production, and social change.* New York: Teachers College Press.

Gordon, S. P. (2008). *Collaborative action research: Developing professional learning communities.* New York: Teachers College Press.

Goswami, D., Lewis, C., Rutherford, M., & Waff, D. (2009). *Teacher inquiry: Approaches to language and literacy research.* New York: Teachers College Press.

Gottfried, A. E., Fleming, J. S., & Gottfried, A. W. (2001). Continuity of academic intrinsic motivation from childhood through late adolescence: A longitudinal study. *Journal of Educational Psychology, 93*(1), 3–13.

Graham, S., & Perin, D. (2007). *Writing next: Effective strategies to improve writing of adolescents in middle and high schools: A report to Carnegie Corporation of New York.* Washington, DC: Alliance for Excellent Education.

Greenleaf, C. L., & Hinchman, K. (2009). Reimagining our inexperienced adolescent readers: From struggling, striving, marginalized, and reluctant to thriving. *Journal of Adolescent and Adult Literacy, 53*(1), 4–13.

Greenleaf, C. L., Jimenez, R., & Roller, C. (2002). Reclaiming secondary reading interventions: From limited to rich conceptions, from narrow to broad conversations. *Reading Research Quarterly, 37*(4), 484–496.

Greenleaf, C. L., Schoenbach, R., Cziko, C., & Mueller, F. (2001). Apprenticing adolescent readers to academic literacy. *Harvard Educational Review, 71*(1), 79–129.

Gregory, G., & Kuzmich, L. (2005). *Differentiated literacy strategies for student growth and achievement in grades 7–12.* Thousand Oaks, CA: Corwin.

Gresham, F. (2001, August). *Response to Intervention: An alternative approach to the identification of learning disabilities.* Paper presented at the Learning Disabilities Summit: Building a Foundation for the Future, Washington, DC.

Gresham, F., Restori, A., & Cook, C. (2008, September). To test or not to test: Issues pertaining to response to intervention and cognitive testing. *Communique, 37,* 5–7.

Guibert, E. (2008). *Alan's war: The memories of G.I. Alan Cope.* Wellington, Australia: First Edition.

Guthrie, J. T. (1996). Educational contexts for engagement in literacy. *The Reading Teacher, 49*(6), 432–445.

Guthrie, J. T. (2008). *Engaging adolescents in reading.* Thousand Oaks, CA: Corwin.

Guthrie, J. T., & Davis, M. (2003). Motivating struggling readers in middle school through an engagement model of classroom practice. *Reading & Writing Quarterly, 19*(1), 59–85.

Gutierrez, K., Morales, P. Z., & Martinez, D. (2009). Re-mediating literacy: Culture, difference, and learning for students from non-dominant communities. *Review of Research in Education, 33*(1), 213–245.

Guzzetti, B., Elliott, K., & Welsch, D. (2010). *DIY media in the classroom.* New York: Teachers College Press.

Hagood, M. C., Alvermann, D. E., & Heron-Hruby, A. (2010). *Bring it to class: Unpacking pop culture in literacy learning.* New York: Teachers College Press.

Hall, L. (2005). Teachers and content area reading: Attitudes, beliefs and change. *Teaching and Teacher Education, 21*(4), 403–414.

Harmon, J. M. (2000). Creating contexts for supporting word meaning constructions:

Dialogues with struggling middle school readers. In T. Shannahan & F. V. Rodriguez-Brown (Eds.), *49th Yearbook of the National Reading Conference* (pp. 331–343). Chicago: National Reading Conference.

Harmon, J. M. (2002). Teaching independent word learning strategies to struggling readers. *Journal of Adolescent and Adult Literacy, 45*(7), 606–615.

Harmon, J. M., Hedrick, W. B., & Wood, K. D. (2005). Research on vocabulary instruction in the content areas: Implications for struggling readers. *Reading and Writing Quarterly, 21*(3), 261–280.

Harry, B., & Klingner, J. (2007). Discarding the deficit model. *Educational Leadership, 64*(5), 16–21.

Hasbrouck, J. E., & Tindal, G. A. (2006). Oral reading fluency norms: A valuable assessment tool for reading teachers. *The Reading Teacher, 59*(7), 636–644.

Hawkins, M. R. (2004). Researching English language and literacy development in schools. *Educational Researcher, 33*(3), 14–25.

Heller, R., & Greenleaf, C. (2007). *Literacy instruction in the content areas: Getting to the core of middle and high school improvement.* Washington, DC: Alliance for Excellent Education.

Heron, A. H. (2003). A study of agency: Multiple constructions of choice and decision making in an inquiry-based summer school program for struggling readers. *Journal of Adolescent and Adult Literacy, 46*(7), 568–579.

Heshusius, L. (1995). Listening to children: "What could we possibly have in common?" From concerns with self to participatory consciousness. *Theory Into Practice, 43*(2), 117–123.

Hinchman, K., Alvermann, D., Boyd, F., Brozo, W. G., & Vacca, R. (2003/2004). Supporting older students' in- and out-of-school literacies. *Journal of Adolescent and Adult Literacy, 47*(4), 304–310.

Hock, M. F., & Deshler, D. D. (2003). Don't forget the adolescents. *Principal Leadership, 4*(3), 50–56.

Hull, G., & Schultz, K. (2002). *School's out! Bridging out-of-school literacies with classroom practice.* New York: Teachers College Press.

IRA Commission on RTI. (2009, February/ March). Working draft of guiding principles. *Reading Today, 26*(4), 6. Retrieved May 2, 2009, from http://www.reading.org/General/Publications/ReadingToday/RTY-0902-rti.aspx

Irvine, J. J., & Fraser, J. W. (1998). Warm demanders. *Education Week, 17*(35), 56–57.

Ivey, G. (1999a). A multicase study in the middle school: Complexities among young adolescent readers. *Reading Research Quarterly, 34*(2), 172–192.

Ivey, G. (1999b). Reflections on teaching struggling middle school readers. *Journal of Adolescent and Adult Literacy, 42*(5), 372–381.

Ivey, G., & Baker, M. (2004). Phonics instruction for older students? Just say no. *Educational Leadership, 61*, 35–39.

Jacobson, J., Thrope, L., Fisher, D., Lapp, D., Frey, N., & Flood, J. (2001). Cross-age tutoring: A literacy improvement approach for struggling adolescent readers. *Journal of Adolescent and Adult Literacy, 44*(6), 528–537.

Jetton, T. L., & Dole, J. A. (Eds.). (2004). *Adolescent literacy research and practice.* New York: Guilford.

Jiménez, R. T., & Teague, B. L. (2007). Legitimacy, recognition, and access to language and literacy: English language learners at the secondary school level. In L. S. Rush, J. Eakle, & A. Berger (Eds.), *Secondary school literacy: What research reveals for classroom practices* (pp. 165–183). Urbana, IL: National Council of Teachers of English and the National Conference on Research in Language and Literacy.

Johnson, E., Mellard, D. F., Fuchs, D., & McKnight, M. A. (2006). *Responsiveness to Intervention (RTI): How to do it.* Lawrence, KS: National Research Center on Learning Disabilities.

Johnson, E. S., & Smith, L. (2008). Implementation of response to intervention at middle school: Challenges and potential benefits. *Teaching Exceptional Children, 40*(3), 46–52.

Johnson, M., & Pleece, W. (2009). *Incognegro.* London: Titan.

Johnston, P. H. (1987). Teachers as evaluation experts. *The Reading Teacher, 40*(8), 744–748.

Jones, D. L. (2009). *Analyzing the effects of two response to intervention tools, oral reading fluency and Maze assessments, in the language arts classrooms of middle school students* [doctoral dissertation]. Retrieved November 15, 2010, from http://digitalcommons.liberty.edu/cgi/viewcontent.cgi?article=1261&context=doctoral

Kamil, M. L., Borman, G. D., Dole, J., Kral, C. C., Salinger, T., & Torgesen, J. (2008). *Improving adolescent literacy: Effective classroom and intervention practices: A practice guide* [NCEE#2008-4027]. Washington, DC: National Center for Educational Evaluation and Regional Assistance, Institute of Education Sciences, U.S. Department of Education. Retrieved November 7, 2010, from http://ies.ed.gov/ncee/wwc

Kavale, K., Kauffman, J., Bachmeier, R., & LeFever, G. (2008). Response-to-Intervention: Separating the rhetoric of self-congratulation from the reality of specific learning disability identification. *Learning Disability Quarterly, 31*(3), 135–150.

Kintsch, E. (2005). Comprehension theory as a guide for the design of thoughtful questions. *Topics in Language Disorders, 25*(1), 51–65.

Kintsch, W., & Kintsch, E. (2005). Comprehension. In S. Paris & S. Stahl (Eds.), *Current issues on reading comprehension and assessment* (pp. 71–92). Mahwah, NJ: Erlbaum.

Kohn, A. (2007, May 31). NCLB: Too destructive to salvage. *USA Today.* Retrieved January 17, 2010, from http://blogs.usatoday.com/oped/2007/05/opposing_view_t.html

Kovaleski, J. F. (2003, December). *The three tier model of identifying learning diabilities: Critical program features and system issues.* Paper presented at the Responsiveness-to-Intervention symposium of the National Research Center on Learning Disabilities, Kansas City, MO.

Krashen, S. (2004). *The power of reading: Insights from the research* (2nd ed.). Portsmouth, NH: Heinemann.

Krashen, S. (2008). Bogus claims about Reading First. *Rethinking Schools, 22*(3), 32–33. Retrieved November 19, 2010, from http://www.rethinkingschools.org/archive/22_03/bogu223.shtml

Kuhn, M. R., & Stahl, S. A. (2003). Fluency: A review of developmental and remedial practices. *Journal of Educational Psychology, 95*(1), 3–21.

Kungner, J. K., & Edwards, P. A. (2006). Cultural considerations with Response to Intervention models. *Reading Research Quarterly, 41*(1), 108–117.

Laird, J., DeBell, M., Kienzl, G., & Chapman, C. (2007). *Dropout rates in the United States: 2005*. Washington, DC: National Center for Educational Statistics.

Langer, J. A. (2002). *Effective literacy instruction: Building successful reading and writing programs*. Urbana, IL: National Council of Teachers of English.

Langer, J. A. (2004). *Getting to excellent: How to create better schools*. New York: Teachers College Press.

Lankshear, C., & Knobel, M. (2002). Do we have your attention? New literacies, digital technologies, and the education of adolescents. In D. Alvermann (Ed.), *Adolescents and literacies in a digital world* (pp. 19–39). New York: Peter Lang.

Lankshear, C., & Knobel, M. (2004). *A handbook for teacher research: From design to implementation*. London: Open University Press.

Leander, K. (2002). Locating Latanya: The situated production of identity artifacts in classroom interaction. *Research in the Teaching of English, 37*(2), 198–250.

Lee, C. D. (1997). Bridging home and school literacies: Models for culturally responsive teaching, a case for African American English. In J. Flood, S. B. Heath, & D. Lapp (Eds.), *Handbook of research on teaching literacy through the communicative and visual arts* (pp. 334–345). New York: Macmillan.

Lee, P. W. (1999). In their own voices: An ethnographic study of low-achieving students within the context of school reform. *Urban Education, 34*(2), 214–244.

Lesley, M. (2004). Looking for critical literacy with postbaccalaureate content area literacy students. *Journal of Adolescent & Adult Literacy, 48*(4), 320–334.

Lester, J. H. (2000). Secondary instruction: Does literacy fit in? *High School Journal, 83*(3), 10–16.

Leu, D. J., Jr. (2002, February). Internet workshop: Making time for literacy. *The Reading Teacher, 55*(5), 466–472. Retrieved October 4, 2010, from http://www.readingonline. org/electronic/elec_index.asp?HREF=/ electronic/RT/2-02_Column/index.html

Madelaine, A., & Wheldall, K. (2004). Curriculum-based measurement of reading: Recent advances. *International Journal of Disability, Development and Education, 51*(1), 57–82.

Marshall, K. (2006). *Interim assessments: Keys to successful implementation*. Retrieved January 17, 2006, from http://www. marshallmemo.com/articles/Interim%20 Assmt%20Report%20Apr.%2012%2006. pdf

Marzano, R. (2005). *Preliminary report on the 2004–2005 evaluation study of the ASCD program for building academic vocabulary*. Alexandria, VA: Association of Supervision and Curriculum Development. Retrieved October 17, 2007, from www. ascd.org/ASCD/pdf/Building%20 Academic%20Vocabulary%20Report.pdf

Marzano, R. J., & Pickering, D. J. (2005). *Building academic vocabulary*. Alexandria, VA: Association for Supervision and Curriculum Development.

Mastropieri, M. A., & Scruggs, T. E. (2005). Feasibility and consequences of response to intervention: Examination of the issues and scientific evidence as a model for the identification of individuals with learning disabilities. *Journal of Learning Disabilities, 38*(6), 525–531.

Mastropieri, M. A., Scruggs, T., Mohler, L., Beranek, M., Spencer, V., Boon, R., & Talbott, E. (2001). Can middle school students with serious reading difficulties help each other and learn anything? *Learning Disabilities Research, 16*(1), 18–27.

McCarthy, S. J., & Moje, E. B. (2002). Identity matters. *Reading Research Quarterly, 37*(2), 228–238.

McCook, J. D. (2006). *The RTI guide: Developing and implementing a model in your schools*. Horsham, PA: LRP Publications.

McCormick, S. (1994). A nonreader becomes a reader: A case study of literacy acquisition by a severely disabled reader. *Reading Research Quarterly, 29*(2), 157–176.

McCormick, S., & Becker, E. Z. (1996). Word recognition and word identification: A review of research on effective instructional practices with learning disabled students.

Reading Research and Instruction, 36(1), 5–17.

McCoss-Yergian, T., & Krepps, L. (2010). Do teacher attitudes impact literacy strategy implementation in content area classrooms? *Journal of Instructional Pedagogies, 4*, 1–18.

McCray, A. D., Vaughn, S., & Neal, L. I. (2001). Not all students learn to read by third grade: Middle school students speak out about their reading disabilities. *Journal of Special Education, 35*(1), 17–30.

McDonald, T., & Thornley, C., Staley, R., & Moore, D. (2009). Research connections: The San Diego Striving Readers' Project: Building academic success for adolescent readers. *Journal of Adolescent and Adult Literacy, 52*(8), 720–722.

McEneaney, J., Lose, M. K., & Schwartz, R. M. (2006). A transactional perspective on reading difficulties and Response to Intervention. *Reading Research Quarterly, 41*(1), 117–128.

McGill-Franzen, A., Payne, R. L., & Dennis, D. V. (2010). Responsive intervention: What is the role of appropriate assessment? In P. Johnston (Ed.), *RTI in literacy: Responsive and comprehensive* (pp. 115–128). Newark, DE: International Reading Association.

McQuillan, J., & Au, J. (2001). The effect of print access on reading frequency. *Reading Psychology, 22*(3), 225–248.

Mellard, D., & Johnson, E. (2008). *RTI: A practitioner's guide to implementing response to intervention*. Thousand Oaks, CA: Corwin.

Mellard, D., Layland, D., & Parsons, B. (2008). *RTI at the secondary level: A review of the literature*. Lawrence, KS: National Center on Response to Intervention.

Mertens, S. B., & Flowers, N. (2004). *NMSA research summary #21: Interdisciplinary teaming*. Retrieved October 3, 2010, from www.nmsa.org/portals/0/pdf/publications/On_Target/teaming/teaming_6_research21.pdf

Moje, E. B. (2002). Re-framing adolescent literacy research for new times: Studying youth as a resource. *Reading Research and Instruction, 41*(3), 211–228.

Moje, E. B. (2008). Foregrounding the disciplines in secondary literacy teaching and learning: A call for change. *Journal of Adolescent and Adult Literacy, 52*(2), 96–107.

Moje, E. B., Callazo, T., Carrillo, R., & Marx, R. (2001). "Maestro, what is 'quality'"? Language, literacy, and discourse in project-based science. *Journal of Science Teaching, 38*(4), 469–496.

Moje, E. B., McIntosh Ciechanowski, K., Kramer, K., Ellis, L., Carrillo, R., & Collazo, T. (2004). Working toward third space in content area literacy: An examination of everyday funds of knowledge and discourse. *Reading Research Quarterly, 39*(1), 38–70.

Moore, D. W. (1996). Contexts for literacy in secondary schools. In D. J. Leu, C. K. Kinzer, & K. A. Hinchman (Eds.), *Literacies for the 21st century: Research and practice* (45th yearbook of the National Reading Conference, pp. 15–46). Chicago: National Reading Conference.

Morrell, E. (2002). Toward a critical pedagogy of popular culture: Literacy development among urban youth. *Journal of Adolescent and Adult Literacy, 46*(1), 72–77.

Morris, D., Ervin, C., & Conrad, K. (1996). A case study of middle school reading disability. *The Reading Teacher, 49*(5), 368–377.

Mraz, M., Rickelman, R. J., & Vacca, R. T. (2009). Content-area reading: Past, present, and future. In K. Wood & W. Blanton (Eds.), *Literacy instruction for adolescents: Research-based practice* (pp. 77–91). New York: Guilford.

Naglieri, J. A. (2007). RTI alone is not sufficient for SLD identification: Convention presentation by OSEP Director Alexa Posny. *Communiqué, 35*(5), 52–53.

Nagy, W. E., McLure, E. F., & Montserrat, M. (1997). Linguistic transfer and the use of context by Spanish-English bilinguals. *Applied Psycholinguistics, 18*(4), 431–452.

Nagy, W. E., & Scott, J. A. (2000). Vocabulary processes. In M. Kamil, P. Mosenthal, P. D. Pearson, & R. Barr (Eds.), *Handbook of reading research* (Vol. III, pp. 269–284). Mahwah, NJ: Erlbaum.

National Assessment of Educational Progress. (2010). *The nation's report card: Reading 2009*. Retrieved December 10, 2010, from http://nces.ed.gov/pubsearch/pubsinfo.asp?pubid=2010458

National Association of State Directors of Special Education. (2007). *Myths about RTI*. Retrieved September 10, 2010, from www.nasdsc.org

National Center for Education Statistics. (2010). *The condition of education 2010* [NCES 2010-028, Indicator 5]. (1979–2008). Retrieved December 2, 2010, from http://nces.ed.gov/fastfacts/display.asp?id=16

National Clearinghouse for English Language Acquisition (NCELA). (2010). Frequently asked questions. Retrieved December 2, 2010, from http://www.ncela.gwu.edu/faqs/

National Council of Teachers of English. (2004). *A call to action: What we know about adolescent literacy and ways to support teachers in meeting students' needs.* Urbana, IL: Author.

National Council of Teachers of Mathematics. (2000). *Principles and standards for school mathematics.* Reston, VA: Author.

National Education Summit on High Schools. (2005). *An action agenda for improving America's high schools.* Retrieved June 11, 2009, from http://www.achieve.org/SummitActionAgenda

National Reading Panel. (2000). *Teaching children to read.* Retrieved April 22, 2004, from http://www.nichd.nih.gov/publications/nrp/upload/smallbook_pdf.pdf

Neild, R. C. (2009). Falling off track during the transition to high school: What we know and what can be done. *The Future of Children, 19*(1), 53–76.

Neild, R. C., Stoner-Eby, S., & Furstenburg, F. (2008). Connecting entrance and departure: The transition to ninth grade and high school dropout. *Education and Urban Society, 40*(5), 543–569.

O'Brien, D., Stewart, R., & Moje, E. (1995). Why content literacy is difficult to infuse into the secondary school: Complexities of curriculum, pedagogy, and school culture. *Reading Research Quarterly, 30,* 442–463.

O'Brien, D. G. (2001). "At-risk" adolescents: Redefining competence through the multiliteracies of intermediality, visual arts, and representation. *Reading Online, 4*(11). Retrieved October 17, 2010, from http://www.readingonline.org/newliteracies/lit_Index.asp?HREF=/newliteracies/obrien/index.html

Ogle, D. M., & Hunter, K. (2001). Developing leadership in literacy at Amundsen High School: A case study of change. In M. Bizar & R. Barr (Eds.), *School leadership in times of urban reform* (pp. 179–194). Mahwah, NJ: Lawrence Erlbaum.

Organisation for Economic Co-Operation and Development. (2001). *Knowledge and skills for life: First results from PISA 2000.* Paris: Author.

Organisation for Economic Co-Operation and Development. (2010). *Strong performers and successful reformers in education lessons from PISA for the United States.* Retrieved December 8, 2010, from http://dx.doi.org/10.1787/9789264096660-en

Padak, N. D., & Rasinski, T. V. (2008). *Evidence-based instruction in reading: A professional development guide to fluency.* New York: Pearson.

Paige, D. (2006). Increasing fluency in disabled middle school readers: Repeated reading utilizing above grade level reading passages. *Reading Horizons, 46*(3), 167–181.

Papalewis, R. (2004). Struggling middle school readers: Successful, accelerating intervention. *Reading Improvement, 41*(1), 24–37.

Park, T. D., & Osborne, E. (2006). Agriscience teachers' attitudes toward implementation of content area reading strategies. *Journal of Agriculture Education, 47*(4), 39–51.

Pearson, P. D., Hiebert, E. H., & Kamil, M. L. (2007). Vocabulary assessment: What we know and what we need to learn. *Reading Research Quarterly, 42*(2), 282–296.

Plaut, S. (2009). *The right to literacy in secondary schools: Creating a culture of thinking.* New York: Teachers College Press.

Polakow, V., & Brozo, W. G. (1994). Deconstructing the at-risk discourse: Power, pedagogy, and the politics of inequity [Special section editors' introduction]. *The Review of Education, 15*(3/4), 217–221.

Rakes, T. A., & Smith, L. J. (1992). Assessing reading skills in the content areas. In E. Dishner, T. Bean, J. Readence, & D. Moore (Eds.), *Reading in the content areas: Improving classroom instruction* (pp. 145–159). Dubuque, IA: Kendall/Hunt.

Rampey, B. D., Dion, G. S., & Donahue, P. L. (2009). *The nation's report card: Trends in academic progress in reading and mathematics 2008.* Retrieved June 11, 2009, from http://nces.ed.gov/nationsreportcard/pubs/main2008/2009479.asp

RAND Reading Study Group. (2002). *Reading for understanding: Toward an R&D program in reading comprehension*. Santa Monica, CA: RAND.

Rasinksi, T., Padak, N. D., McKeon, C., Wilfong, L. G., Friedauer, J. A., & Helm, P. (2005). Is reading fluency a key for successful high school reading? *Journal of Adolescent and Adult Literacy, 48*(1), 22–27.

Rasinski, T., Retzel, R., Chard, D., & Linan-Thompson, S. (2011). Fluency. In M. Kamil, P. Pearson, E. Moje, & P. Afflerbach (Eds.), *Handbook of reading research* (Vol. IV, pp. 286–319). Mahwah, NJ: Erlbaum.

Reschly, D. (2005, August). RTI paradigm shift and the future of SLD diagnosis and treatment. Paper presented to the Annual Institute for Psychology in the Schools of the American Psychological Association, Washington, DC.

Reynolds, C. R., & Shaywitz, S. E. (2009). Response to Intervention: Ready or not? Or, From wait-to-fail to watch-them-fail. *School Psychology Quarterly, 24*(2), 130–145.

Ruiz-de-Velasco, J., Fix, M., & Clewell, B. C. (2001). *Overlooked and underserved—Immigrant students in U.S. secondary schools: Core findings and conclusions*. Retrieved January 15, 2010, from http://www.urban.org/pdfs/overlooked.pdf

Samuels, C. A. (2009). High schools try out RTI. *Education Week, 28*(19), 20–22.

Samuels, S. J. (2002). Reading fluency: Its development and assessment. In A. E. Farstrup & S. J. Samuels (Eds.), *What research has to say about reading instruction* (3rd ed., pp. 166–183). Newark, DE: International Reading Association.

Santa, C. M. (2006). A vision for adolescent literacy: Ours or theirs? *Journal of Adolescent and Adult Literacy, 49*(6), 466–476.

Scammacca, N., Roberts, G., Vaughn, S., Edmonds, M., Wexler, J., Reutebuch, C. K. et al. (2007). *Reading interventions for adolescent struggling readers: A meta-analysis with implications for practice*. Portsmouth, NH: RMC Research Corporation, Center on Instruction.

Scanlon, D. M., & Anderson, K. L. (2010). Using the interactive strategies approach to prevent reading difficulties in an RTI context. In M. Lipson & K. Wixson (Eds.), *Successful approaches to RTI: Collaborative practices for improving K–12 literacy* (pp. 21–65). Newark, DE: International Reading Association.

Schultz, K. (2002). Looking across space and time: Reconceptualizing literacy learning in and out of school. *Research in the Teaching of English, 36*(3), 356–390.

Scott, J. A., Jamieson-Noel, D., & Asselin, M. (2003). Vocabulary instruction throughout the day in twenty-three Canadian upper-elementary classrooms. *The Elementary School Journal, 103*(3), 269–286.

Shanahan, T., & Shanahan, C. (2008). Teaching disciplinary literacy to adolescents: Rethinking content area literacy. *Harvard Educational Review, 78*(1), 40–59.

Shanklin, N. (2008). At the crossroads: A classroom teacher's key role in RTI. *Voices from the Middle, 16*(2), 62–63.

Shaywitz, S. E. (2008). Foreword. In E. Fletcher-Janzen & C. R. Reynolds (Eds.), *Neuropsychological perspectives on learning disabilities in the era of RTI: Recommendations for diagnosis and intervention* (p. xi). New York: Wiley.

Shinn, M. (1989). *Curriculum-based measurement: Assessing special children*. New York: Guilford.

Shinn, M. (1998). *Advanced applications of curriculum-based measurement*. New York: Guilford.

Shinn, M. (2007). Identifying students at risk: Monitoring performance and determining eligibility within response to intervention: Research on educational need and benefit from academic intervention. *School Psychology Review, 36*(4), 638–646.

Shultz, J., & Cook-Sather, A. (2001). *In our own words: Students' perspectives on school*. Lanham, MD: Rowman & Littlefield.

Stanovich, K. E., & Cunningham, A. E. (1993). Where does knowledge come from? Specific associations between print exposure and information acquisition. *Journal of Educational Psychology, 85*(2), 211–229.

Stecker, P. M. (2007). Tertiary intervention. *Teaching Exceptional Children, 39*(5), 50–57.

Stecker, P. M., & Fuchs, L. S. (2000). Effecting superior outcomes using curriculum-based measurement: The importance of individual progress monitoring. *Learning Disabilities Research and Practice, 15*(3), 128–143.

Strangeman, N., Hitchcock, C., Hall, T., Meo, G., & Coyne, P. (2006). *Response-to-Instruction and universal design for learning: How might they intersect in the general education classroom?* Washington, DC: The Access Center.

Strickland, D., & Alvermann, D. E. (Eds.). (2004). *Bridging the literacy achievement gap, grades 4–12.* New York: Teachers College Press.

Strong, A. C., Wehby, J. H., Falk, K. B., & Lane, K. L. (2004). The impact of a structured reading curriculum and repeated reading on the performance of junior high students with emotional and behavioral disorders. *School Psychology Review, 33*(4), 561–581.

Stroud, K. C., & Reynolds, C. R. (2009). Assessment of learning strategies and related constructs in children and adolescents. In T. Gutkin & C. R. Reynolds (Eds.), *The handbook of school psychology* (4th ed.). New York: Wiley.

Sturtevant, E., Boyd, F., Brozo, W., Hinchman, K., Alvermann, D., & Moore, D. (2006). *Principled practices for adolescent literacy: A framework for instruction and policy.* Mahwah, NJ: Lawrence Erlbaum.

Sturtevant, E. G. (2003). *The literacy coach: A key to improving teaching and learning in secondary schools.* Retrieved September 10, 2010, from http://www.all4ed.org/publications/reports.html

Sugai, G. (2004, May). *Schoolwide positive behavior support in high schools: What will it take?* Paper presented at the Illinois High School Forum of Positive Behavioral Interventions and Supports, Naperville, Illinois.

Sunderman, G. L., Kim, J. S., & Orfield, G. (2005). *NCLB meets school realities: Lessons from the field.* Thousand Oaks, CA: Corwin.

Supovitz, J. A., & Weinbaum, E. H. (2008). *The implementation gap: Understanding reform in high schools.* New York: Teachers College Press.

Tatum, A. (2008). Toward a more anatomically complete model of literacy instruction: A focus on African American male adolescents and texts. *Harvard Educational Review, 78*(1), 155–180.

Taylor, B., Frye, B., & Maruyama, G. (1990). Time spent reading and reading growth. *American Educational Research Journal, 27*(2), 351–362.

Tilly, W. D., Reschly, D. J., & Grimes, J. (1999). Disability determination in problem-solving systems: Conceptual foundations and critical components. In D. Reschly, W. Tilly, & J. Grimes (Eds.), *Special education in transition* (pp. 221–251). Longmont, CO: Sopris West.

Tomlinson, C. A. (2001). *How to differentiate instruction in mixed-ability classrooms* (2nd ed.). Alexandria, VA: Association for Supervision and Curriculum Development.

Tomlinson, C. A. (2004). The mobius effect: Addressing learner variance in schools. *Journal of Learning Disabilities, 37*(6), 516–524.

Tomlinson, C. A. (2005). Differentiating instruction in the middle grades: Why bother? *Middle Ground, 9*(1), 12–14.

Tomlinson, C. A., Brighton, C., Hertberg, H., Callahan, C., Moon, T., Brimijoin, K., Conover, L., & Reynolds, T. (2004). Differentiating instruction in response to student readiness, interest, and learning profile in academically diverse classrooms: A review of literature. *Journal for the Education of the Gifted, 27*(2/3), 119–145.

Tractenberg, R. E. (2002). Exploring hypotheses about phonological awareness, memory, and reading achievement. *Journal of Learning Disabilities, 35*(5), 407–424.

Troia, G. (2006). Meaningful assessment of content-area literacy for youth with and without disabilities. *Assessment for Effective Intervention, 31*(2), 69–80.

U.S. Department of Education. (2004). *Building the legacy: IDEA 2004.* Washington, DC: Author. Retrieved June 21, 2007, from: http://idea.ed.gov/explore/view/p/%2Croot%2Cregs%2C300%2CD%2C300%252E307%2C

Vacca, R. (1998). Let's not marginalize adolescent literacy. *Journal of Adolescent & Adult Literacy, 41*(8), 604–609.

Vaughn, S., & Fuchs, L. S. (2003). Redefining learning disabilities as inadequate response to intervention: The promise and potential problems. *Learning Disabilities Research and Practice, 18*(3), 137–146.

Vaughn, S., & Klingner, J. (2007). Overview of the three-tier model of reading intervention. In E. Haager, J. Klingner, & S. Vaughn (Eds.), *Evidence-based reading practices for response to intervention* (pp. 3–10). Baltimore, MD: Brookes.

Vaughn, S., & Linan-Thompson, S. (2003). What is special about special education for students with learning disabilities? *Exceptional Children, 69*(4), 391–409.

Vaughn, S., Linan-Thompson, S., & Hickman, P. (2003). Response to treatment as a means of identifying students with reading/learning disabilities. *Exceptional Children, 69*(4), 391–409.

Vaughn, S., Mathes, P. G., Linan-Thompson, S., & Francis, D. (2005). Teaching English language learners at risk for reading disabilities to read: Putting research into practice. *Learning Disabilities Research and Practice, 20*(1), 58–67.

Vaughn, S., Moody, S. W., & Schumm, J. S. (1998). Broken promises: Reading instruction in the resource room. *Exceptional Children, 64*(2), 211–225.

Wasley, P. A., Hampel, R. L., & Clark, R. W. (1997). *Kids and school reform.* San Francisco: Jossey-Bass.

Wassell, B. A., Hawrylak, M. F., & LaVan, S. K. (2010). Examining the structures that impact English language learner's agency in urban high schools: Resources and roadblocks in the classroom. *Education and Urban Society, 42*(5), 599–619.

Wedl, R. (2005). *Response to intervention: An alternative to traditional eligibility criteria for students with disabilities.* Center for Policy Studies and Hamline University. Retrieved November 28, 2009, from http://www.educationevolving.org/pdf/Response_to_Intervention.pdf

Wilson, M. (2005). *Constructing measures: An item response modeling approach.* Mahwah, NJ: Erlbaum.

Wilson, N., Grisham, D., & Smetana, L. (2009). Investigating content area teachers' understanding of a content literacy framework: A yearlong professional development initiative. *Journal of Adolescent and Adult Literacy, 52*(8), 708–718.

Wright, J. (2007). *RTI toolkit: A practical guide for schools.* Port Chester, NY: National Professional Resources.

Ysseldyke, J. E., & Marston, D. (1999). Origins of categorical special education services in schools and a rationale for changing them. In D. Reschly, W. D. Tilly III, & J. Grimes (Eds.), *Special education in transition: Functional assessment and noncategorical programming* (pp. 1–18). Longmont, CO: Sopris West.

Ysseldyke, J. E., Thurlow, M. L., Mecklenburg, C., & Graden, J. (1984). Opportunity to learn for regular and special education students during reading instruction. *Remedial and Special Education, 5*(1), 29–37.

Yudowitch, S., Henry, L. M., & Guthrie, J. T. (2008). Self-efficacy: Building confident readers. In J. Guthrie (Ed.), *Engaging adolescents in reading* (pp. 66–82). Thousand Oaks, CA: Corwin.

Zirkel, P. A. (2006). *SLD eligibility: A user's guide to the new regulations.* Lawrence, KS: National Research Center on Learning Disabilities. Retrieved September 10, 2010, from www.nrcld.org

Zirkel, S. (2002). Is there a place for me? Role models and academic identity among white students and students of color. *Teachers College Record, 104*(2), 357–376.

Index

Accelerated Reader program, 63–64
ACT, 1
Acuity® program, 135, 137
Adequate yearly progress (AYP), 31–32
Adolescence. See also Secondary education
  adolescents as resource in RTI, 55–57,
    111–112, 118–119, 125–126
  complexity of, 45–48
  educational change literature and, 46
  slump during, 45–46
  as stage of development, 45
Afflerbach, P. P., 13, 25, 83, 101
AIMSWEB-MAZE, 117, 118
Alan's War (Guibert), 93
Alger, C., 38
Allington, Richard L., vii, 3, 21, 52, 58, 62,
    76, 77, 99, 107, 134–139, 143
Alvermann, D. E., 27, 39, 43, 51, 74, 76, 87,
    103, 119, 122, 128–129, 138, 140, 141
Alwell, M., 4, 48
Anderman, E. M., 45–46
Anders, P., 26
Anderson, K. L., 52
Applebaum, M., 12, 19
Archer, A. L., 86, 97
Army Men (3DO), 90
Asselin, M., 68
Assessment
  acquiring regular feedback on student
    reading and learning, 67–73
  determining literacy abilities of all
    students, 62–67
  in RTI, 12–16, 62–73
  words correct per minute (WCPM), 16,
    97–98
Au, J., 76–77

Bachmeier, R., 132–134, 142–143
Baer, D. M., 10
Baker, M., 59, 87, 101, 114
Barnet, D., 16
Barnett, D. W., 8
Baskette, M. R., 17
Batsche, G. M., 3, 18
Becker, E. Z., 101
Beers, K., 76, 95, 101
Behavior analysis in education, 10
Belfanz, Robert, 27–28
Bender, W. N., 16, 17
Ben's Guide to U.S. Government for Kids
    site, 84, 98
Beranek, M., 58
Best, R., 84
Bhattacharya, A., 86
Biancarosa, G., 38, 40, 46, 74, 76, 113, 139
Blevins, W., 86, 98
Block 21 grants, 135
Block scheduling, 32–35
Board on Children, Youth, and Families, 46
Bomer, R., 57
Boon, R., 58
Borman, G. D., 46
Boyd, F., 27, 43, 74, 76, 103, 128, 138, 141
Bradley, R., 9
Braunger, J., 40
Brighton, C., 127
Brimijoin, K., 127
Brown-Chidsey, R., 16
Brozo, C. L., 52
Brozo, William G., 8, 12, 13, 17, 24–27, 38–
    40, 43, 45–47, 52, 55–57, 60, 61, 63, 65, 70,
    74–77, 80, 83, 99, 101, 103, 111, 112, 123,
    125, 126, 128, 138, 140–142

Bubble maps, 72–73
Buchanan, C. M., 45–46
Buddy readers, 88–91
Busch, T. W., 71
Bush, George W., 20, 134
Butkus, Dick, 89

Calhoon, M. B., 27
California English Language Development
    Test (CELDT), 123
California Standards Test-English
    Language Arts (CST-ELA), 123
Callahan, C., 127
Callazo, T., 126, 141
Camilli, G., 62
Cantrell, S. C., 40
Cappella, E., 46, 58, 77
Carney, J. J., 99
Carrillo, R., 56, 126, 130, 141
Cases in RTI, 106–130
    Cheyenne Mountain Junior High School,
        78–79
    Chicopee Public Schools (Massachusetts),
        14–15
    Green Middle School, 29, 31–35, 42–45,
        47–48
    Heritage High School, 28–31, 38, 40–42,
        47–48
    Liberty Middle School (Virginia), 108–115
    Lincoln Public Schools (Nebraska),
        115–123
    Portland Public Schools (Oregon), 36–37
    San Diego Unified School District
        (California), 123–129
    Springfield Public Schools
        (Massachusetts), 14–15
    Western Greenbrier Middle School,
        135–138
Cassidy, D., 3
Cassidy, J., 3
Chapman, C., 2
Chard, D., 16
Chem4Kids site, 98
Cheyenne Mountain Junior High School
    (case), 78–79
Chicopee Public Schools (case;
    Massachusetts), 14–15
Choral reading, 100

Cioffi, G., 99
Cipielewski, J., 76
Clark, R. W., 47, 56
Clewell, B. C., 25
Cloze/maze passages, 68, 69
Cobb, B., 4, 48
Coburn, C. E., 75
Collazo, T., 56, 130
Common Core State Standards Initiative
    (CCSI), 141–142
Community partners as reading mentors,
    91–95
Compton, D., 9
Computer games, 90
Conley, M. W., 46
Connor, C. M., 9
Conover, L., 127
Conrad, K., 123
Content-area reading inventories, 65–67
Content areas, 95–103
    fluency development in context, 96–100
    word recognition in context, 100–103
Content Enhancement Routines (CERs), 36
Content Literacy Continuum® (CLC),
    108–115
Cook, C., 133
Cook-Sather, A., 24, 46–47, 55, 56
Cooter, R. B., 44
Corbett, H. D., 47, 56
Cortiella, C., 2
Coulter, W. A., 12
Coyne, P., 3
Crawford, A. N., 100
Cross-age tutoring, 88–91
Cunningham, A. E., 101
Curriculum-Based Measurement (CBM),
    12–13, 64–65, 67–73, 83–84
Cziko, C., 39, 59

Daane, M., 57
Dale, E., 99
Daly, E. J., 8, 16
Danielson, L., 9
Davis, M., 45–46
DEAR (Drop Everything and Read), 75
DeBell, M., 2
Degrees of Reading Power (DRP), 36, 123,
    127

Dennis, D. V., 129
Deno, S. L., 10
Deshler, D. D., 3, 40, 57, 74, 76, 113, 133–134, 139
Deshler, R. T., 74
Diagnostic Assessment in Reading (DAR), 78
DIBELS (Dynamic Indicators of Basic Early Literacy Skills), 117, 118, 122
Digital Storytelling software, 89
Dimino, J. A., 9
Dion, G. S., 1
DIRT (Daily Individual Reading Time), 75
Discourse negotiation (Gee), 46–47
Dolch Basic Sight Vocabulary, 98–99
Dole, J. A., 46, 129, 141
Donahue, D., 39, 40
Donahue, P. L., 1, 57
Dong, Y. R., 61
Doolittle, J., 9
Dozier, C., 115
Draper, R. J., 38, 39
Dubay, W., 13, 68
Dudley, A. M., 96
Duffy, H., 3, 19, 26

Early reading interventions, 20–21
Eccles, J. S., 45–46
Echo reading, 100
Edmonds, M., 133
Edwards, P. A., 141
Edyburn, D., 142
Ehren, B. J., 48, 62, 107, 113, 133, 139
Ehri, L. C., 86, 95
Elliott, K., 140
Ellis, L., 56, 130
English for Speakers of Other Languages (ESOL), 54
Erikson, E., 45
Ervin, C., 123
Espin, C. A., 71
Evans, K., 40
Evidence-based instruction, 26, 27, 139–140

Falk, K. B., 13, 96
Fisher, D., 38, 43, 58, 70, 77, 83, 120, 122, 126, 142
Fisher, J., 40
Fix, M., 25

Flanigan, K., 68
Fleming, J. S., 45–46
Fletcher, J. M., 12, 20, 133
Flood, J., 58
Florida Center for Reading Research, 113
Flowers, N., 127
Fluency development, in context, 96–100
Flynt, S., 123
Foegen, A., 71
Foorman, B. R., 20
Francis, D. J., 20, 97
Fraser, J. W., 33
Frey, N., 58, 70, 142
Friedauer, J. A., 96
Frye, B., 76
Fry's Instant Word List, 98–99
Fuchs, D., 2–4, 8, 9, 16, 48, 62, 64, 133–134
Fuchs, L. S., 3, 4, 8, 9, 16, 27, 48, 62, 64
Fullan, M., 46
Furstenburg, F., 46

Galguera, T., 40
Gardiner, S., 76
Gates McGinitie Reading Test (GMRT), 63
Gee, J. P., 45, 46
Gelzheiser, L. M., 74
Gersten, R., 9
Gillet, J. W., 100
Gleason, M. M., 86, 97
Goetze, S. K., 48, 62, 107, 113, 133
Goodman, K., 122
Goodman, L., 70
Goodman, S., 141
Gordon, S. P., 140
Goswami, D., 140
Gottfried, A. E., 45–46
Gottfried, A. W., 45–46
Graden, J., vii
Graff, J., 62
Graham, S., 139
Graphic novels, 92–95
Greenleaf, C. L., 39, 40, 59, 127, 139
Green Middle School (case)
  block scheduling, 32–35
  concerns for student voice and engagement, 47–48
  structural conditions for RTI, 29, 31–35
  support structures for RTI, 42–45

Greenwood, S. C., 68
Gregory, G., 113
Gresham, F., 8–10, 133
Grigg, W., 57
Grimes, J., 10
Group Reading Assessment and Diagnostic
    Evaluation (GRADE), 37
Guibert, E., 93
Guthrie, J. T., 45–46, 87, 119
Gutierrez, K., 56
Guzzetti, B., 140

Hagood, M. C., 140
Halgren-Flynn, L., 74
Hall, K. M., 39
Hall, L., 39
Hall, T., 3
Hampel, R. L., 47, 56
Hargis, C. H., 12, 61, 63, 74, 77, 126
Harmon, J. M., 70, 87, 103
Harry, B., 9
Hasbrouck, J. E., 13, 96
Hawkins, M. R., 25
Hawrylak, M. F., 59, 141–142
Hedrick, W. B., 70
Heller, R., 139
Helm, P., 96
Henry, L. M., 87
Heritage High School (case)
    concerns for student voice and
        engagement, 47–48
    professional development workshops,
        29–30
    school culture, 38
    structural conditions for RTI, 28–31
    support structures for RTI, 40–42
Heron, A. H., 127
Heron-Hruby, A., 140
Hertberg, H., 127
Heshusius, L., 47, 56
Hickman, P., 16
Hiebert, E. H., 70
High-frequency words, 98–99
Hinchman, K. A., 27, 43, 46, 74, 76, 103, 127,
    128, 138, 141
Hitchcock, C., 3
Hock, M. F., 57
Hughes, H. K., 40

The Hulk (Vivendi-Universal), 90
Hull, G., 130, 141
Hunter, K., 75

Incognegro (Johnson & Pleece), 93–94
Individualized Educational Plan (IEP), 19, 92
Individuals with Disabilities Education Act
    (IDEA), 2, 8–9, 17, 20–21, 25, 73–74, 77,
    86, 120, 139
International Reading Association
    Commission on RTI, 3–5, 20–21
Iowa Test of Basic Skills (ITBS), 116, 117, 122
Irvine, J. J., 33
Ivey, G., 38, 59, 70, 77, 83, 87, 101, 114, 120,
    122, 123

Jacobson, J., 58
Jamieson-Noel, D., 68
Jetton, T. L., 129, 141
Jiménez, R. T., 40, 59
Johns, N., 4, 48
Johnson, D., 12
Johnson, E. S., 16, 27, 48
Johnson, M., 93–94
Johnston, P. H., 122–123
Jones, D. L., 13
Jones, K. M., 8
Jordan, Michael, 89

Kamil, M. L., 46, 70
Kauffman, J., 132–134, 142–143
Kavale, K., 132–134, 142–143
Kienzl, G., 2
Kim, J. S., 25
Kintsch, E., 84
Kintsch, W., 84
Klingner, J., 9, 58
Knobel, M., 140
Kohn, A., 25
Kovaleski, J. F., 17
Kral, C. C., 46
Kramer, K., 56, 130
Krashen, S., 75, 76, 97, 114, 139
Krepps, L., 39
Kruschwitz, R., 71
Kuhn, M. R., 96
Kungner, J. K., 141
Kuzmich, L., 113

Laird, J., 2
Lane, K. L., 13, 96
Langer, J. A., 40, 44, 75, 76, 126
Lankshear, C., 140
Lapp, D., 58
Laster, B., 48, 62, 107, 113, 133
LaVan, S. K., 59, 141–142
Layland, D., 27
Leadership
  in school culture, 74–75
Leander, K., 126
LEARN Act, 2
Learning disabled students (LD)
  alternative to, 9
  characteristics of, vii
  classification of, vii, 8–9
  extent of, 8–9
Least restrictive environment, 28
Lee, C. D., 130, 141
Lee, P. W., 47, 56
LeFever, G., 132–134, 142–143
Lentz, F. E., 8
Lester, J. H., 39
Leu, D. J., Jr., 64
Lewis, C., 140
Liberty Middle School (case; Virginia),
  108–115
Linan-Thompson, S., vii, 9, 16, 97
Lincoln Public Schools (case; Nebraska),
  115–123
Lindamood Phoneme Sequencing program
  (LiPS), 137
Living Word Vocabulary, The (Dale &
  O'Roarke), 99
Lord, S., 45–46
Lose, M. K., 139–140

Madelaine, A., 13, 68
Maehr, M. L., 45–46
Marshall, K., 12
Marston, D., 8
Martens, B. K., 16
Martinez, C., 56
Maruyama, G., 76
Marx, R., 126, 141
Marzano, R. J., 68, 99
Mastropieri, M. A., 9, 27, 58
Mathes, P. G., 97

Maze tasks, 13–16, 68, 69, 117, 118
McCarthy, S. J., 45, 127
McCook, J. D., 19
McCormick, S., 101, 123
McCoss-Yergian, T., 39
McCray, A. D., 25
McDonald, T., 124
McEneaney, J., 139–140
McGill-Franzen, A., vii, 62, 129
McIntosh Ciechanowski, K., 56, 130
McKeon, C., 96
McKnight, M. A., 16
McLure, E. F., 101
McMahon, Jim, 89
McNamara, D., 84
McQuillan, J., 76–77
Mecklenburg, C., vii
Mediasphere (O'Brien), 140
Mehta, P., 20
Mellard, D. F., 12, 16, 27
Mentoring programs, 91–95
Meo, G., 3
Mertens, S. B., 127
Midgley, C., 45–46
Mock, D., 2, 8, 133
Mohler, L., 58
Moje, E. B., 37–39, 45, 51, 56, 126, 127, 130,
  141
Monteserrat, M., 101
Moody, S. W., vii
Moon, T., 127
Moore, D. W., 27, 39, 43, 74, 76, 103, 124,
  128, 138
Morales, P. Z., 56
Morgan, P. L., 2, 8, 133
Morrell, E., 125, 141
Morris, D., 123
Mraz, M., 39, 142
Mueller, F., 39, 59
Mulhall, P. F., 127

Naglieri, J. A., 133
Nagy, W. E., 68, 101
Nair, M., 76, 113
National Assessment of Educational
  Progress (NAEP), 1, 57, 134
National Association of State Directors of
  Special Education (NASDE), 77

National Center for Education Statistics, 141

National Clearinghouse for English Language Acquisition (NCLEA), 141

National Council of Teachers of English (NCTE), 59

National Council of Teachers of Mathematics (NCTM), 67–68

National Education Summit on High Schools, 2, 24–25

National Reading Panel, 59, 95–96, 96, 121

Neal, L. I., 25

Nebraska State Writing Test (NeSA-W), 116, 117, 122

Neild, R. C., 27, 46

Nelson Denny Reading Test (NDRT), 63

No Child Left Behind (NCLB), 2, 25, 40, 95, 121

Nowak, R., 62

Nuves, S., 95

O'Brien, D. G., 37, 39, 51, 122, 140

Ogle, D. M., 75

Olson, S. C., 16

Oral Reading Fluency (ORF), 13–16

Oregon Scholastic Aptitude Test (OSAT), 36–37

Orfield, G., 25

Organisation for Economic Co-Operation and Development (OECD), 2, 134

O'Roarke, J., 99

OSAT (Oregon Scholastic Aptitude Test), 36–37

Osborne, E., 40

Ozuru, Y., 84

Padak, N. D., 96, 100

Paige, D., 27

Palincsar, A. S., 76, 113

Papalewis, R., 27

Park, T. D., 40

Parsons, B., 27

PASS Act, 2

Payne, R. L., 129

Payton, Walter, 89

Pearson, P. D., 70

Perin, D., 139

Perry, "Fridge," 89

Phonics, 20, 59, 86–87, 95

Phonological awareness, 20

Pickering, D. J., 99

Pinchback, Zane, 93–94

PISA (Program for International Student Assessment), 1, 134

Plaut, S., 38

Pleece, W., 93–94

Polakow, V., 52

Portland Public Schools (case; Oregon), 36–37

Problem-Solving Team (PST), 78

Probst, R., 76

Process guides, 84–85

Professional Learning Communities, 135–136

Program for International Student Assessment (PISA), 1, 134

Progress monitoring, in RTI, 12–16. *See also* Assessment

Public Law 94-142, 8, 9

Puckett, K. S., 40, 141

Rakes, T. A., 65

Rampey, B. D., 1

RAND Reading Study Group, 70

Rasinski, T. V., 16, 96, 100

Readers' theater, 100

Reading Cyclone, 76

Reading failure prevention, 77–86
  at whole-class level, 80–82
  within-class differentiated instruction, 82–86

Reading First, 2–3, 20

Reading mentors, community partners as, 91–95

Reading Next (Biancarosa & Snow), 139

Read 180®, 14–15, 109, 112, 113, 114–115, 118, 120

Relate to Integrate, 144

Repeated readings, 99–100

Reschly, D. J., 10, 12, 133

Resistance to intervention, 10

Response to Intervention (RTI) approach
  achieving comprehensive and responsive programs at secondary level, 61–73

adolescents as resource in, 55–57, 111–112, 118–119, 125–126
adopting, 2
as alternative to IQ discrepancy method, 2
benefits of, 22
cases. *See* Cases in RTI
challenges and criticisms, 22, 23–49, 132–134
components of, 12–21
within comprehensive literacy programs, 57–58, 112, 119–120, 126
creation of, vii
described, 2–3
designing and implementing, 3
effective teachers in, 60–61, 115, 122–123, 128–129
envisionments of, 53–61
expanding student literacy capacities at all levels, 73–86
guidelines for use, 134–142
history of, 8–12
meeting needs of students with serious reading difficulties, 86–103
as model in search of validation, 8
more than curriculum of basic skills redux, 58–59, 113–115, 121–122, 127
moving from elementary to secondary and special education to general education, 19–21
opinions about inception, 10
preservation and improvement of, 134–142
preventing reading failure, 77–86
principles of, 55–61, 87, 111–115, 118–123, 125–129
as problem-solving approach, 10–12
Relate to Integrate, 144
as responsive literacy instruction, 50–52
school culture, 37–39, 74–77
special supports but not always special settings in, 58, 112–113, 120–121, 126–127
structural conditions for, 28–37
for struggling adolescent readers, 24–26
support structures, 39–45
teacher identity, 37–39

Tier 1, vii, 14, 16–18, 24, 30, 36, 38, 74, 78, 117, 121, 124, 133, 136, 137
Tier 2, 14, 16–17, 18, 30–31, 36–37, 38, 79, 117–118, 120–121, 124, 126–127, 129, 133, 136, 137
Tier 3, 14, 17, 19, 30–31, 38, 79, 120–121, 133, 135–137
tiered interventions, vii, 14, 16–19
utility of, 3–4
Restori, A., 133
Retzel, R., 16
Reutebuch, C. K., 133
Reynolds, C. R., 3, 132, 134, 139
Reynolds, T., 127
Rickelman, R. J., 39, 142
Rief, L., 76
Risley, T. R., 10
Roberts, G., 133
Roller, C., 40, 59
Rowe, M., 84
RTI. *See* Response to Intervention (RTI) approach
Ruiz-de-Velasco, J., 25
Rush, L. S., 122
Rutherford, M., 140

Salinger, T., 46
Sample, P., 4, 48
Samuels, C. A., 27
Samuels, S. J., 99
San Diego Quick Assessment of Reading Ability, 136
San Diego Unified School District (case; California), 123–129
Santa, C. M., 142
Santoro, L., 9
Scammacca, N., 133
Scanlon, D. M., 52, 74
Schatschneider, C., 20
Schoenbach, R., 39, 59
Scholastic Reading Inventory (SRI), 110–111, 136–137
School culture, 37–39, 74–77
Schultz, K., 130, 141
Schumaker, J., 40
Schumm, J. S., vii
Schwartz, R. M., 139–140
Scott, J. A., 68

Scruggs, T. E., 9, 27, 58
Secondary education. *See also* Adolescence
    achieving comprehensive and responsive
        programs at secondary level, 61–73
    complexity of, 26–28
    complexity of adolescence, 45–48
    guidelines for use of RTI, 134–142
    literacy reform in, 76–77
    meeting needs of students with serious
        reading difficulties, 86–103
    Response to Intervention (RTI) approach
        in, 19–21. *See also* Response to
        Intervention (RTI) approach
    structural conditions for RTI, 28–37
Serious reading difficulties, 86–103
    community partners as reading mentors,
        91–95
    cross-age tutoring, 88–91
    teaching basic skills in context, 95–103
Shanahan, C., 80, 101, 141
Shanahan, T., 80, 101, 141
Shanklin, N., 20
Shaywitz, S. E., 3, 132–134, 139
Shiel, G., 112
Shin, J., 71
Shinn, M., 10, 13, 16
Shores, C., 16, 17
Shultz, J., 47, 56
Sieber, D., 39
Sight words, 98–99
Simpson, M. L., 25, 38, 40, 52, 57, 65, 75, 80,
    125, 138
Skateboard Science site, 53
Smith, L., 27, 48
Smith, L. J., 65
Smith, L. K., 39
Snoop Dogg, 102–103
Snow, C., 38, 40, 46, 139
Spencer, V., 58
Springfield Public Schools (case;
    Massachusetts), 14–15
Stahl, S. A., 95, 96
Staley, R., 124
Stanford Diagnostic Reading Rest, 4th
    edition (SDRT-4), 14
Stanovich, K. E., 76, 101
STAR tests, 63–64
Stecker, P. M., 16, 19
Steege, M. W., 16

Stewart, R., 37, 39
Stoner-Eby, S., 46
Strangeman, N., 3
Strategic Model Content Enhancement
    Routines for Teachers (SIM-CERT), 14,
    36–37, 109–110
Strategies for Literacy Independence across
    the Curriculum (SLIC) model, 124–127
Strickland, D., 129, 141
Striving Readers project, 123–124
Strong, A. C., 13, 96
Stroud, K. C., 139
Student Assistance Period (SAP), 113
Student Questions for Purposeful Reading
    (SQPR), 81–82
Sturtevant, E. G., 27, 43, 74–76, 103, 128, 138
Sugai, G., 27
Sunderman, G. L., 25
Supovitz, J. A., 26, 74–75
Sustained silent reading (SSR), 48, 75–77,
    97–98, 126
Sustained Uninterrupted Reading for Fun
    (SURF), 137
System 44™, 118, 120, 122

Take No Prisoners (Red Orb), 90
Talbott, E., 58
Tatum, A., 40
Taylor, B., 76
Teague, B. L., 40
Temple, C., 100
Test of Reading Comprehension (TORC),
    116
Test of Written Language (TOWL), 116
Texas Adolescent Literacy Academies
    (TALA), 132–133
Thornley, C., 124
Thrope, L., 58
Thurlow, M. L., vii
Tier 1, in Response to Intervention (RTI)
    approach, vii, 14, 16–18, 24, 30, 36, 38,
    74, 78, 117, 121, 124, 133, 136, 137
Tier 2, in Response to Intervention (RTI)
    approach, 14, 16–17, 18, 30–31, 36–37,
    38, 79, 117–118, 120–121, 124, 126–127,
    129, 133, 136, 137
Tier 3, in Response to Intervention (RTI)
    approach, 14, 17, 19, 30–31, 38, 79, 120–
    121, 133, 135–137

Tilly, W. D., 9, 10
Tindal, G. A., 13, 96
Tomlinson, C. A., 17, 127, 142
Topping, K., 112
Torgesen, J. K., 20, 46
Tractenberg, R. E., 13, 96
Troia, G., 67
True Crime (Activision), 90
Tutoring, cross-age, 88–91

Ulmer, L., 17
U.S. Department of Education, 2, 123
Universal screening, 12–16, 62
University of California, Berkeley, 123, 124
University of Kansas Center for Research
    on Learning
    Content Literacy Continuum® CLC),
      108–115
    Strategic Instruction Model (SIM)
      Content Literacy Curriculum, 14,
      36–37, 109–110
Urlacher, Brian, 89

Vacca, R. T., 26, 39, 57, 74, 128, 141, 142
Vachon, V. L., 86, 97
Vaughn, S., vii, 8, 12, 16, 25, 58, 97, 133
Vocabulary matching, 71–72
Vocabulary self-assessment, 68–71

Waff, D., 140
Wait and fail approach, 77
Walmsley, S. A., 3
Wasley, P. A., 47, 56
Wassell, B. A., 59, 141–142
Webquests, 53
Wedl, R., 10

Wehby, J. H., 13, 96
Weinbaum, E. H., 26, 74–75
Weinstein, R., 46, 58, 77
Welsch, D., 140
Western Greenbrier Middle School (case),
    135–138
WESTEST 2, 135–136
Wexler, J., 133
Wheldall, K., 13, 68
Wilfong, L. G., 96
Williams, L., 62
Willows, D., 95
Wilson, M., 124
Wilson, R. L., 47, 56
Wilson Reading Program, 109, 112, 113, 118
Wilson Reading System, 137
Witt, J. C., 16
Wolf, M. M., 10
Wood, K. D., 70
Word recognition, in context, 100–103
Words correct per minute (WCPM), 16,
    97–98
Word study, 86–87
Wright, J., 10
WWF Wrestlemania (THQ), 90

X-Men (Activision), 90
Xtreme Reading, 14, 15, 36–37

Young, C. L., 2, 8, 133
Ysseldyke, J. E., vii, 8
Yudowitch, S., 87

Zeig, J., 62
Zirkel, P. A., 73–74, 121
Zmach, C., 62

About the Author

William G. Brozo is a Professor of Literacy in the Graduate School of Education at George Mason University in Fairfax, Virginia. He earned his bachelor's degree from the University of North Carolina and his master's and doctorate from the University of South Carolina. He has taught reading and language arts in the Carolinas. He is the author of numerous books and articles on literacy development for children and young adults, and is a contributing author to Prentice-Hall Literature, a program for adolescent readers. He serves on the editorial review board of the *Journal of Adolescent & Adult Literacy*, was past columnist of "Strategic Moves" for the international journal *Thinking Classroom*, and currently authors the "Content Literacy" column for *The Reading Teacher*. He is a past member of IRA's Commission on Adolescent Literacy, a current member of the Adolescent Literacy Committee, and chair of the PISA/PIRLS Task Force, an international team of scholars. As an IRA-USAID consultant, Dr. Brozo has traveled frequently to the Balkans and currently to Oman, where he provides technical support to secondary teachers. He is currently a member of a European research grant team developing curriculum and providing adolescent literacy professional development for teachers in Southern and Eastern Europe. He also speaks regularly at professional meetings around the country and consults with states and districts on ways of building capacity among teacher leaders, enriching the literate culture of schools, enhancing the literate lives of boys, and making teaching more responsive to the needs of all students.